The 2030 Agenda and the Death of Freedom

By
Benjamin Hunter

The 2030 Agenda and the Death of Freedom

Table of Contents

Introduction

A s we edge closer to 2030, the world finds itself teetering on the precipice of monumental change. This isn't just an evolution of policies or a shift in political climate; it's a reconfiguration of the very fabric of society. The agenda set forth for 2030 is painted with broad strokes of idealism, promising global unity and sustainable development. But beneath its polished veneer lies a framework that could potentially reorient how we live, think, and even perceive our freedoms.

The 2030 Agenda, also known as Agenda 2030, is an ambitious plan adopted by the United Nations in 2015. It's aimed at addressing a wide spectrum of global challenges—from poverty and hunger to climate change and inequality. Its 17 Sustainable Development Goals (SDGs) serve as the roadmap for countries around the world to achieve a better and more sustainable future. However, the intricacies and implications of these goals raise significant questions about individual autonomy and freedoms.

Comprehending the full scope of the 2030 Agenda requires us to traverse through layers of strategic objectives, political maneuvers, and economic frameworks. One striking aspect is its potential to centralize power, thereby shifting the balance from individual sovereignty to institutional control. This shift isn't just theoretical. Various components of the agenda advocate for robust mechanisms of governance and oversight. For some, this signifies a step towards a more coordinated and unified world. For others, it's a harbinger of overreaching control and diminished freedoms.

We must also consider the role of influential organizations and figures that are driving this agenda forward. Entities like the World Economic Forum (WEF) and individuals like Klaus Schwab champion the notion of a 'Great Reset'—a paradigm shift where traditional models of ownership and economic participation are redefined. It's a future where, ostensibly, you will own nothing and be happy. Such ideas challenge our conventional understanding of personal ownership and economic liberty, sowing seeds of concern about who truly benefits from these changes.

The United Nations, the orchestrator of this grand vision, is not merely an international body but a powerful player influencing global policies. The centralized nature of its agenda necessitates a scrutiny of global governance structures and their implications. How much control should unelected bodies hold over national and individual decisions? The answers to these questions are neither simple nor straightforward.

Then there are national governments and politicians who align themselves with Agenda 2030, another layer of complexity. Take Canada, for example. Canadian politicians have been vocal supporters of the agenda, integrating its principles into domestic policies. This alignment raises critical questions about national sovereignty and the role of elected officials in representing the interests of their citizens while adhering to international frameworks.

As we navigate through this intricate web of policies and principles, privacy emerges as a front-line concern. The advent of digital identification systems, often touted as a means to streamline services and enhance security, also opens doors to potential invasions of privacy. How much personal data should be accessible to governments and corporations? What safeguards exist to protect this information from misuse?

In parallel, financial systems are undergoing a radical transformation. Governments are increasingly exploring Central Bank Digital Currencies (CBDCs), systems that could provide unparalleled oversight and control over financial transactions. While these might offer benefits like security and efficiency, they also pose significant risks to financial freedom. We have to ask ourselves: Are these changes a gateway to innovation, or do they pave the way for unprecedented control?

No discussion on control mechanisms would be complete without addressing the concept of social credit systems. These systems, which score individuals based on various behaviors and interactions, are already in place in countries like China. The implications of such scoring systems extend beyond mere numbers; they influence access to services, travel, and even social standing. The prospect of a global social credit system stirs apprehension about a future where personal freedom is dictated by algorithms.

Surveillance has become a ubiquitous part of modern life. From smartphones to smart homes, technology companies harvest vast amounts of data, ostensibly to improve user experience. But the line between convenience and intrusion is thin. The extent of citizen surveillance raises fundamental questions about privacy and autonomy in the digital age. How much are we willing to sacrifice for convenience?

As this narrative unfolds, it is imperative to consider the resistance movements and activism emerging in response to this agenda. Legal battles and constitutional rights are the battlegrounds where individual liberties are defended. Such challenges highlight the importance of awareness and advocacy. The fight against overreach isn't just about curbing policies but about preserving the very essence of personal freedom.

This book seeks to unravel the complexities and implications of the 2030 Agenda. It delves into the potential consequences for daily life, personal freedom, and economic independence. Through analytical exposition and journalistic investigation, we aim to present a comprehensive understanding of why this agenda could be scarier than it appears at first glance.

As we proceed, remember that understanding is the first step towards action. Equipped with knowledge and awareness, you can better navigate the impending changes and advocate for a future that respects individual freedoms. This isn't just a look into a distant future; it's a call to engage with the present to shape what lies ahead.

Chapter 1:
The 2030 Agenda: An Overview

The year 2030 is more than just a date on a calendar. It's a deadline for an elaborate agenda set forth by world leaders, aiming to reshape the social and economic fabric of our lives. This agenda, commonly known as the 2030 Agenda, presents itself as a blueprint for a sustainable and equitable world. But beneath its veneer of noble intentions lies a series of implications that could fundamentally alter our lives.

At its core, the 2030 Agenda comprises 17 Sustainable Development Goals (SDGs), which are further divided into 169 targets. These goals encompass everything from eradicating poverty and hunger to promoting clean energy and combating climate change. The language used is alluring: sustainability, equity, inclusiveness. Yet, it's essential to understand the mechanics behind these grandiose plans to grasp the far-reaching consequences they entail.

The seeds of the 2030 Agenda were planted at the United Nations Sustainable Development Summit in 2015. Attended by member states from across the globe, the summit sought to address the world's pressing issues through collective action. The SDGs were crafted to guide global efforts and national policies, but the scope and scale of these efforts warrant scrutiny.

One of the fundamental aspects of the 2030 Agenda is its holistic approach. It doesn't isolate issues but instead interlinks various social, economic, and environmental dimensions. This interconnectedness aims to break down silos, ensuring that improvements in one area complement advances in another. However, this interdependence also means that a failure in one domain could have ripple effects across the entire framework.

Moreover, the 2030 Agenda calls for unprecedented levels of cooperation between governments, businesses, NGOs, and civil society. While this seems collaborative, it raises questions about sovereignty and autonomy. Are nations and their citizens ready to cede control over their economic and social policies to a global framework? And if so, what are the potential consequences of such a cession?

Another key aspect to consider is the financial commitment the 2030 Agenda demands. Achieving these ambitious goals requires substantial investment, projected to be in trillions of dollars. The funding sources for these investments are varied, including public finance, private sector contributions, and international aid. The financial burden is colossal, and the way it will be distributed remains a point of concern.

Of equal importance is the governance structure surrounding the 2030 Agenda. The United Nations and various international bodies play critical roles in monitoring and guiding the implementation of the SDGs. These institutions are often perceived as distant and bureaucratic, and their influence over national policies can be both profound and intrusive. The relationship between these global entities and sovereign nations is a delicate balance of power.

In examining the 2030 Agenda, one cannot overlook the narrative driving it. The underlying vision is one of universal well-being, equality, and sustainability. But this vision can be interpreted in different ways, often leading to contentious debates. Critics argue that the agenda, while noble in rhetoric, masks a more insidious push towards centralized control and loss of individual freedoms.

In summary, the 2030 Agenda is a complex and ambitious blueprint for global transformation. Its goals and targets are sweeping, its vision grandiose. However, the ramifications of its implementation are profound and multifaceted. Understanding the agenda is the first step towards critically evaluating its potential impacts on our lives and freedoms. As we dive deeper into this book, the layers behind these lofty goals will be peeled back, revealing the true stakes involved.

Understanding the Agenda

Before diving into the complexities of the 2030 Agenda, it's vital to grasp its overarching goals and motivations. The 2030 Agenda, officially known as the United Nations' 2030 Agenda for Sustainable Development, is a comprehensive framework signed by all member states of the United Nations in 2015. It aims to address some of the world's most pressing issues, like poverty, inequality, and climate change, by setting forth 17 Sustainable Development Goals (SDGs) to be achieved by the year 2030.

At its core, the 2030 Agenda presents a vision of a world where sustainable development is paramount. These SDGs encompass a broad range of objectives intended to improve societal conditions on a global scale. From ending poverty and hunger to fostering peaceful, inclusive societies, these goals cover an extensive array of targets that touch upon nearly every aspect of life.

While the vision appears noble on the surface, understanding what lies beneath is equally crucial. Achieving these goals requires nations to align their policies and actions in unprecedented ways. This alignment often translates into sweeping changes in national regulations, governance structures, and economic policies. The broad nature of these goals raises questions about the extent to which individual freedoms and national sovereignties might be compromised in the name of global unity.

Critical to understanding the agenda is recognizing its top-down approach to governance. The UN and other supranational entities dictate the course for individual nations, guiding them toward a collective future. This centralized control has been a point of contention, with critics arguing that it erodes local governance and infringes on personal liberties. Autonomy is traded for uniformity, and the diverse needs of individual nations can get lost in the global shuffle.

Another essential aspect is how the agenda interprets development. The concept of sustainability goes beyond environmental concerns, encompassing economic and social dimensions. While this holistic approach is beneficial in theory, it brings with it sweeping mandates that influence a nation's internal affairs. For instance, sustainability in economic terms often implies a push for global economic integration, which can lead to reduced barriers for financial capital but increased barriers for individuals regarding personal decision-making.

The mechanics of implementing this global vision require massive financial and intellectual resources. International bodies like the World Bank and the International Monetary Fund become critical players, often dictating terms and conditions for funding that tie nations to global objectives. This financial dependency adds another layer of control, nudging nations to comply with broader agendas lest they risk economic isolation or financial distress.

Equally significant is the agenda's emphasis on data and metrics. Progress toward the SDGs is meticulously recorded, requiring extensive data collection across various sectors. While transparency and accountability are commendable goals, the implications of such widespread data gathering pose severe privacy concerns. National and individual data are harvested on an enormous scale, often stored and analyzed by entities beyond national jurisdictions.

Understanding the agenda also means acknowledging the role of non-state actors. Organizations, corporations, and even influential individuals play substantial roles in pushing the 2030 Agenda forward. These entities work alongside governments, sometimes with more significant influence and resources than the states themselves. This dynamic creates a complex web of interests, where public goals might be swayed by private agendas.

The social paradigm advocated by the 2030 Agenda also deserves a closer look. It aims to reshape societal norms and behaviors profoundly. The push for inclusive education, gender equality, and peacebuilding is enshrined in the SDGs, but these lofty aims come with their own set of challenges. Social engineering on such a scale requires widespread acceptance and compliance, which can conflict with traditional values and national cultures.

In essence, the 2030 Agenda is about creating a unified world with shared goals. While the promise of a better future is appealing, the path to achieving it is fraught with potential sacrifices of autonomy, privacy, and individual freedoms. These are not small trade-offs, and understanding their implications is critical for anyone looking to comprehend the full breadth of what the 2030 Agenda entails.

It is still vital to scrutinize the real-world impacts and the specific ways in which these large-scale goals translate into everyday life. This understanding helps in anticipating how the transformative promises of the 2030 Agenda can dramatically alter our current ways of living, governance, and personal freedoms.

As we delve deeper into the subsequent chapters, each aspect of the agenda will come into sharper focus, revealing just how integrated and pervasive this vision for 2030 aims to be. This chapter serves as a foundation to grasp the essentials of the agenda before we dissect its individual components and their broader impacts.

The Vision Behind the Goal

The 2030 Agenda is steeped in grand notions and sweeping transformations. At its core, the vision reaches beyond mere policy changes or legislative efforts. It aims to reshape the very fabric of global society. This holistic overhaul doesn't just target economies or governments; it extends to the daily lives and freedoms of individuals everywhere.

The architects of the 2030 Agenda envision a world where sustainability and equality take precedence over individual freedoms and economic competition. While these goals sound noble, the vision can be unsettling when scrutinized closely. The concept of sustainability within the agenda often translates into strict and direct controls over resources, with far-reaching implications for personal autonomy and national sovereignty.

A significant part of this vision is rooted in redefined metrics of success and well-being. The agenda measures progress not through economic freedom or personal ownership, but through collective outcomes and prescribed standards. This fundamental shift challenges the very essence of personal liberty. One can argue it sets a dangerous precedent, where individual rights may be sacrificed for the "greater good."

Embedded within this vision is an unprecedented level of global governance. Organizations like the United Nations and the World Economic Forum play crucial roles in shaping and enforcing these global standards. This kind of top-down management, where decisions are made by a select few, raises essential questions about democracy, representation, and accountability.

Another cornerstone of the 2030 vision is the notion of equity. By equity, the agenda does not merely mean equal opportunity, but often implies equal outcomes. Achieving such an aim requires engineered interventions that control various aspects of life. These interventions span income redistribution, limitations on private enterprises, and stringent environmental regulations. While the aspiration is to bridge gaps and uplift the marginalized, the methodologies proposed risk stifling innovation, initiative, and personal ambition.

In pursuing this vision, technology is seen both as a tool and a monitoring mechanism. Innovations like Digital IDs and Central Bank Digital Currencies (CBDCs) propose a tightly controlled financial system. These tools, if not carefully constrained, could lead to an Orwellian landscape where every transaction is tracked, and financial autonomy is stripped away. The implications on privacy and personal freedom are profound and alarming.

The global emphasis on collective goals often threatens to blur the distinction between public good and individual rights. Policies influenced by this outlook tend to lean towards collectivism, which could pave the way for a slippery slope where the state intervenes in more aspects of daily life. This vision for the future features rigid societal structures that restrict personal choices in an attempt to create uniformity and compliance.

This centralized vision of governance and economic management is not without its critics. Skeptics argue that such a model inherently risks ignoring the diverse needs and values of different communities and cultures. By aiming for a unilateral approach, the unique contexts and perspectives that vary from country to country could be marginalized.

Moreover, the notion of a digital society envisioned by the 2030 Agenda introduces the specter of comprehensive surveillance. Digital tracking and social credit systems, for instance, are heralded as advancements for security and efficiency. Yet, they also hold the potential for misuse, turning into mechanisms for control and repression. The fine line between safeguarding public interest and infringing on personal freedom becomes increasingly blurred within this framework.

The aspiration to build a utopian society through the 2030 Agenda ignores some fundamental human elements — the desire for personal space, the right to dissent, and the need for spontaneous, unscripted actions. Bureaucratic overreach, in the name of environmental and economic goals, could breed a stifling atmosphere where creative expression and entrepreneurial spirit are constrained.

Economic implications are equally troubling. The path outlined by the 2030 vision often entails disrupting traditional market forces and introducing new regulatory frameworks. This could lead to unintended economic consequences that might include reduced competitiveness, job losses, and stifled innovation.

Despite the intention to create a harmonious global society, the journey to achieve the goals of the 2030 Agenda is fraught with complexities and potential pitfalls. Implementing such an expansive vision requires not only immense political will but also the acquiescence of global citizens who might not fully understand or agree with every aspect.

The underpinnings of the 2030 vision suggest a future where governance, economics, and even social contracts are fundamentally transformed. Whether this transformation results in a utopia or a dystopia depends significantly on the interpretation and implementation of these ambitious goals. The balance between collective welfare and individual rights remains a contentious and critical point of debate.

The vision behind the 2030 Agenda thus stands as a hopeful yet cautionary tale. It elucidates the grand possibilities of global unity and progress, while equally opening doors to overreach, control, and loss of essential freedoms. As the world watches and participates in this transformative venture, continuous vigilance, critical analysis, and active involvement are paramount to safeguard personal liberties amid the fervor for collective advancement.

Chapter 2:
The Great Reset: You Will Own
Nothing and Be Happy

The Great Reset. It's a term that has permeated discussions in recent years, stirring both hope and fear in the hearts of many. Unlike previous economic shifts, this isn't merely about tweaking existing structures. Instead, it's a fundamental reimagining of capitalism itself. The architects of this reset envision a future where traditional notions of ownership are rendered obsolete. The mantra, "You will own nothing and be happy," encapsulates a radical departure from the past century's economic models.

Let's start with the basics. The concept of The Great Reset emerged prominently during the COVID-19 pandemic. When economies ground to a halt, the vulnerabilities of the current system were laid bare. Proponents argue that the pandemic offered a unique opportunity to rebuild systems in a more sustainable, equitable way. At its core, The Great Reset seeks to address systemic inequalities and environmental challenges by overhauling the way we live, work, and interact with the natural world.

Yet, what does this mean for personal ownership? That's where things get controversial. Traditional forms of property ownership, be it homes, cars, or even smaller items, would be replaced by communal or shared resources. Imagine a world where you no longer own your home but instead have the right to use communal living spaces. Your car? Forget it. You'll rely on shared mobility solutions. The shift is profound, asking us to embrace a different kind of happiness detached from material possessions.

This vision, while innovative, has raised alarm bells. Skeptics argue that stripping individuals of ownership could lead to a loss of autonomy and personal freedom. In the current system, ownership equates to security and contorl over one's destiny. When you own something, you have the power to make decisions regarding its use, its future, and its protection. Under the new dispensation, these freedoms could be significantly curtailed.

Advocates counter that the focus will shift from ownership to access. Who needs to own a car when you can summon one with a click? Why own a home when you can live anywhere on demand? The Great Reset champions argue that such a system would free people from the burdens of debt and maintenance, allowing them to live more fulfilling lives. They believe that untethering from material possessions will foster deeper community ties and environmental stewardship.

The ultimate goal, they claim, is not to imprison people in a web of shared commodities but to liberate them from the pressure of ownership. Under this scheme, basic needs like housing, transportation, and even some forms of entertainment would be accessible to all, creating what they term "well-being economies." These economies prioritize social and ecological well-being over traditional financial metrics like GDP.

However, real-world applications of such ideas spark concerns about practicality and enforcement. For instance, who decides what constitutes a fair distribution of resources? What safeguards are in place to prevent abuse and ensure equity? These questions linger, posing significant challenges to the feasibility and ethics of The Great Reset.

Another concern lies in the technology that would be necessary to implement such a system. Centralized data collection and digital ID systems would likely be key components. While these technologies promise efficiency and equitable distribution, they also raise significant privacy and security concerns. The potential for misuse is substantial. Could such a system become a tool for unprecedented surveillance and control? The fear is that relinquishing ownership might lead to relinquishing privacy and personal freedoms as well.

It's undeniable that the current economic system has its flaws—rampant inequality, environmental degradation, and volatility to name a few. But the solution proposed by The Great Reset is, at its core, a gamble. It asks us to trade our comfort and security, rooted in ownership, for a promise of communal prosperity. Whether this trade-off will lead to a utopia of shared happiness or a dystopia of lost freedoms remains to be seen.

The Great Reset's vision is audacious, disruptive, and polarizing. It challenges deeply ingrained beliefs about ownership and freedom. In confronting these notions, we must ask ourselves what kind of future we truly want and how much we're willing to sacrifice to achieve it. The promise of happiness without ownership is tantalizing but fraught with questions and risks that demand careful consideration.

The Concept of The Great Reset

At the core of the "Great Reset" lies a vision that suggests profound shifts in our economic, social, and political landscapes, converging on a singular idea: "You will own nothing and be happy." This concept, advocated by the World Economic Forum (WEF) and its founder Klaus Schwab, posits that the conventional notions of ownership and personal property may become obsolete by 2030. Instead, a new paradigm characterized by shared or collective ownership seems to be the end goal. For many, this idea represents a radical departure from centuries-old principles of private property inherent to capitalist economies, raising waves of concern and skepticism.

The proponents of the Great Reset argue that such a transformation is essential for addressing systemic inequities, environmental challenges, and the consequences of technological advancements. They posit that by decoupling ownership from wealth and access, societies can achieve greater equality and sustainability. In practical terms, this might translate into a model where access to goods and services becomes more important than the traditional act of owning them. Think of it as an extension of current trends like the sharing economy, but on a much grander and more all-encompassing scale.

However, the notion of "owning nothing" can be alarming and borderline dystopian for many. Private ownership has long been a keystone of individual liberty and economic freedom. The ability to own property, land, and goods has historically empowered people, allowing them to build wealth, plan for the future, and pass something down to the next generation. Under the Great Reset, this ability could be fundamentally altered or even eradicated, shifting power from individuals to large entities or even governments.

Moreover, skeptics argue that this new model could lead to an increase in centralized control, creating a system where individuals are more dependent on institutions for their daily needs. The concentration of power and resources into the hands of a few could exacerbate the very inequalities the initiative aims to solve. Thus, while the Great Reset promises reforms for a more equitable world, it also threatens to undermine personal freedoms and the sense of autonomy that ownership provides.

One critical aspect of the Great Reset revolves around sustainability and environmental stewardship. Advocates claim that reducing the emphasis on ownership could alleviate ecological pressures by fostering more efficient use of resources. In their vision, a future where goods and services are utilized collectively could mitigate waste and promote a more responsible consumption pattern. For instance, the transition from car ownership to shared mobility services might reduce the number of vehicles on the road, thereby lowering carbon emissions and traffic congestion. While these goals are laudable, their feasibility and implications on everyday life remain contentious topics.

Furthermore, technology plays a pivotal role in actualizing the Great Reset's tenets. Advancements in digital infrastructure, artificial intelligence, and Internet of Things (IoT) applications could facilitate the transition to a "rent-not-own" culture. Smart cities, fueled by connected devices and data analytics, can optimize resource allocation, manage waste effectively, and streamline services for better community living. Yet, such technological reliance brings its own set of issues, especially concerning data privacy and cybersecurity. As individuals increasingly depend on digital platforms and services, safeguarding personal data and maintaining autonomy over one's information becomes paramount.

The Great Reset also touches on economic reinvention. By disassociating ownership from prosperity, proponents argue that economies can be more resilient to shocks such as pandemics or financial crises. The resilience stems from creating a robust system where access to essentials is guaranteed, ostensibly making well-being less tied to fluctuating markets and personal fortunes. However, shifting economic models on such a scale necessitates unprecedented coordination between governments, corporations, and civil society, a feat easier said than done.

Critics of the Great Reset are not only concerned about losing ownership but also about the erosion of personal choice. In a future where individuals are dictated by what they can access rather than what they own, the room for personal decision-making shrinks. Encapsulating choice in the hands of few organizations or state entities introduces the risk of abuse and diminishes the diversity of options available. As history has shown, centralized systems are prone to inefficiencies and exploitation, often failing to cater to the nuanced needs of individuals.

The Great Reset's ambitions underscore a fundamental rethink of how societies function. It foresees a collective, cooperative approach to living, replacing individualism with a shared sense of responsibility. In theory, such a transformation could solve persistent global issues, but whether the practical execution aligns with the ideology is a different question altogether. It also requires a significant cultural shift, away from the deep-seated values that have defined human progress for generations.

In essence, the Great Reset presents a future filled with possibilities and pitfalls alike. It challenges deeply ingrained notions of ownership and personal autonomy, aiming for an equitable and sustainable world. Yet, its conceptual complexity and practical implications invoke a mix of hope and apprehension. As the world grapples with these ideas, the dialogue surrounding the Great Reset becomes more crucial, demanding a fine balance between innovation and preserving hard-won freedoms.

Impacts on Personal Ownership

In the heart of "The Great Reset: You Will Own Nothing and Be Happy," the implications of drastically redefined personal ownership unfold ominously. This shift goes beyond the simple accumulation of material goods; it challenges our very sense of self and autonomy. What does it mean to no longer own anything? The ramifications stretch across multiple facets of daily life, transforming the fundamental relationship between individuals and their belongings.

At the core of this paradigm shift is the idea of shared or collective ownership. Proponents assert that eliminating individual ownership can lead to a more equitable and sustainable society. The theory is rooted in the belief that resources will be better managed collectively, and waste will be significantly reduced. However, stripping individuals of their personal ownership also strips away their autonomy, reducing their ability to make independent choices. In a world where ownership is collectivized, personal freedom is invariably compromised.

Consider the housing market as a prime example. Under the envisioned system, owning a home could become a relic of the past. Instead of individual ownership, people might permanently rent homes or live in communal spaces managed by larger entities. While this model theoretically provides security and reduces the disparities caused by fluctuating property values, it also erodes the personal investment that comes with owning a home. The sense of pride, the financial stability, and the freedom to alter or improve one's living space would be compromised. What happens to personal initiative and ambition in such a scenario?

The impact on personal ownership extends beyond tangible assets. Intellectual property and creative works are also at risk. Will inventors, artists, and writers still be motivated to create when their works might not belong to them individually? The creative economy thrives on the promise of ownership, which is directly tied to reward and recognition. If the fruits of one's labor are not theirs to keep, the drive to innovate and contribute creatively may diminish, stifling human progress.

Moreover, this shift has profound implications for personal privacy. Ownership affords a sphere of individual sovereignty, a space where one's activities, preferences, and thoughts can remain private. When possessions are owned collectively or continuously leased, the line between the individual and the external governing bodies blurs. Surveillance and control become easier for those in power. The dissolution of personal ownership could potentially lead to an environment where every aspect of daily life is monitored, recorded, and regulated.

The question of financial independence also looms large. Personal ownership of assets like cars, homes, and land provides a financial safety net that promotes individual resilience and economic stability. When assets are collectively owned or leased, individuals lack collateral, making it harder to secure loans or withstand financial crises. This sort of dependency can result in increased control by governing bodies over financial decisions, leaving individuals less equipped to navigate economic uncertainties on their own.

Social dynamics also shift in a world where ownership is communal. One of the age-old motivators for societal contribution has been the accumulation of wealth and assets, not just for oneself but for one's family and future generations. When personal ownership diminishes, so too does the driving force behind leaving a legacy. What will motivate society when the ability to bequeath assets to one's descendants is taken away?

The implications stretch into the technological realm as well. Imagine a future where you don't own your smartphone but merely lease it from a conglomerate that retains full control over its functions and data. This not only limits individual control over technological tools but also allows those entities to dictate how these tools are used. When technology isn't truly yours, neither is the data it collects. This places immense power into the hands of few, enabling unprecedented levels of control and surveillance.

Another critical consideration is emotional wellbeing. Ownership isn't just a financial or practical matter; it's an emotional one too. The joy, satisfaction, and sense of achievement derived from owning something valuable—be it a home, a car, or a piece of art—are intrinsic to human experience. This emotional connection to ownership underpins personal identity and self-worth. Removing this fundamental aspect risks creating a society devoid of personal joy and satisfaction, leading to a potential psychological void.

Furthermore, the notion of ownership underpins many of our legal frameworks and rights. Property laws exist to protect individual rights to own, use, and dispose of possessions. Diluting these laws to accommodate a system where personal ownership is obsolete introduces complex legal challenges. How do we redefine property law in a world where property isn't personally owned? And what safeguards will exist to protect individuals from potential abuses of power?

Lastly, the issue of personal ownership touches on deeper philosophical and ethical questions. How do we balance the greater good with individual rights? Can a system that eliminates personal ownership truly respect individual dignity and agency? These are questions that go beyond economics and touch the very core of what it means to be human.

In sum, the impacts on personal ownership in the context of "The Great Reset" are profound and multifaceted. From financial independence and privacy concerns to emotional wellbeing and legal rights, the elimination of personal ownership challenges the very foundations of modern society. As we move forward, understanding these implications isn't just important—it's essential for preserving the core values of freedom, autonomy, and dignity that define human existence.

Chapter 3:
The WEF Klaus Schwab That No One Has Elected

Klaus Schwab. This name has become synonymous with the World Economic Forum (WEF) and its grand vision for the future. Yet, who is this man that sits at the helm of one of the most influential organizations in the world without ever being elected into a position by the masses?

Schwab founded the WEF in 1971, envisioning it as a platform for elite business, political, and intellectual leaders to discuss economic issues. Over the years, the WEF has grown into a behemoth, shaping policies and influencing global agendas. Schwab, with his academic background in economics and engineering, has masterfully steered this organization towards significant power.

Despite his considerable influence, Schwab remains a largely unaccountable figure. The WEF operates behind closed doors, with discussions and decisions often veiled from the public eye. This has led to growing concerns about the transparency and democratic legitimacy of a man who holds so much sway over global policy.

As the architect behind initiatives like The Great Reset and the 2030 Agenda, Schwab's vision extends far beyond economic reform. He envisions a future where societal norms and structures are fundamentally altered, aiming for a more centralized, controlled, and arguably intrusive global order.

The power of the WEF under Schwab's leadership cannot be overstated. The annual Davos meetings attract key figures from all sectors, including governments, multinational corporations, and non-governmental organizations. These interactions have far-reaching implications, affecting national policies and international relations.

Critics argue that the WEF's influence undermines democratic processes. When unelected individuals like Schwab can guide nations towards specific policies, the sovereignty and voice of the people become secondary. The WEF's role in shaping the 2030 Agenda exemplifies this concern, prompting a closer examination of who truly benefits from these global initiatives.

Schwab's narrative often portrays the WEF's mission as benevolent and forward-thinking. However, understanding the implications of such centralized control reveals layers of complexity and potential risks. It's crucial to question whether the vision of one man should direct the future of billions.

While Schwab's ambitions may be rooted in a desire for progress, the pathway to such a future must be scrutinized. The lack of electoral legitimacy and transparency surrounding the WEF invites essential debates about governance, accountability, and the true nature of global leadership.

Who is Klaus Schwab?

Klaus Schwab is a name that many associate with the World Economic Forum (WEF), an organization he founded in 1971. But who is this man who wields so much influence on a global scale? Born in Ravensburg, Germany, in 1938, Schwab studied mechanical engineering and economics. Later, he earned a doctorate in engineering from the Swiss Federal Institute of Technology and a doctorate in economics from the University of Fribourg.

In 1971, Schwab took a significant step by organizing the first European Management Symposium, which later evolved into the World Economic Forum. This annual event held in Davos, Switzerland, brings together global leaders from various sectors to discuss pressing issues facing the world. Schwab envisioned it as a forum where stakeholders from all walks of life—governments, businesses, and civil society—could come together to shape global agendas.

The man behind the WEF isn't just a figurehead who appears once a year. He deeply involves himself in the organization's direction and mission. Schwab has authored several books on the subject of globalization, stakeholder capitalism, and technological change. His 2020 book, "COVID-19: The Great Reset," co-authored with Thierry Malleret, came at a time when the world was grappling with unprecedented challenges due to the pandemic. The book delves into how we could leverage the crisis to build a more resilient, equitable, and sustainable world.

Schwab's influence extends beyond the annual meetings in Davos. He advocates for what he calls "stakeholder capitalism," a model where businesses act not just for their shareholders but for all stakeholders, including employees, communities, and the environment. Proponents argue that this approach could lead to more sustainable and inclusive economic systems. Critics, however, see it as a way for elite figures and corporations to centralize control and undermine democratic institutions.

It's important to note that Schwab has never held an elected office. His power and influence stem from his ability to convene global leaders and shape discourse rather than from a direct mandate given by voters. This lack of electoral accountability raises questions about the legitimacy and transparency of the agendas he promotes.

Documents and leaked communications have revealed that the WEF under Schwab's leadership has significant sway over national policies worldwide. For instance, Schwab's initiative called the "Global Redesign," proposed in the aftermath of the 2008 financial crisis, suggested reforms that would grant more power to multinational corporations and international organizations, often at the expense of national sovereignty.

Schwab's influence is also evident through the WEF's partnerships with numerous global corporations and non-governmental organizations. These partnerships enable the WEF to push its initiatives effectively, making Schwab a pivotal figure in global governance even without an official governmental role. His ideas become embedded in policies and corporate practices, slowly changing the landscape of global economics and politics.

Given his extensive network and the WEF's influence, Schwab has a critical role in driving the 2030 Agenda. His ideas about the Great Reset and stakeholder capitalism align closely with the United Nations' Sustainable Development Goals (SDGs), a key component of the 2030 Agenda. Both frameworks aim at comprehensive changes in society—from environmental sustainability to economic inclusivity—thereby impacting almost every aspect of our daily lives.

As we look at the bigger picture, it's clear that Klaus Schwab's reach goes beyond being just an academic or business leader. His role in the WEF positions him as a nexus of ideas and power that shape global policies, arguably affecting more people than many elected officials ever could. Whether one views him as a visionary seeking to build a better world or as a symbol of elite overreach, his impact on the trajectory of global governance cannot be disputed.

Understanding who Klaus Schwab is gives us a clearer view of the mechanisms driving the 2030 Agenda. His ideas and the WEF's influence are deeply intertwined with the path laid out by this agenda.

This intersection of thought leadership and policy influence is key to grasping the profound changes that could reshape our world in ways many find unsettling.

The Power and Influence of the WEF

The World Economic Forum (WEF) has carved out an unparalleled position in the global arena, permeating the corridors of power with an influence that cannot be overstated. Founded in 1971 by Klaus Schwab, the WEF has skillfully navigated its way to the center of policy-making, acting as a conduit for world leaders, corporate moguls, and intellectuals. Its annual meetings in Davos, Switzerland, have become synonymous with elite discussions, where decisions impacting billions are crafted behind closed doors. How did this organization, one that no one has directly elected, accrue such immense sway?

At its core, the WEF thrives on its ability to bring together disparate actors under the banner of global issues—economic inequality, climate change, and technological advancement, to name a few. This congregation is more than symbolic; it's strategic. The confluence of political clout and financial power creates an ecosystem where ideas are not just discussed but accelerated. While it's easy to frame the WEF as a benign think tank, its role in pushing for the Great Reset reveals a different dimension. The phrase "You will own nothing and be happy" isn't just a tagline but a vision for a future where traditional notions of ownership and freedom are markedly altered.

Moreover, the WEF exerts influence through its vast network. High-profile initiatives like the Global Shapers Community and the Young Global Leaders program act as breeding grounds for future influencers, keen on ideologies aligned with Schwab's vision. These programs are not mere training grounds; they serve to instill a specific worldview, one that dovetails with the Agenda 2030 framework. By fostering a pipeline of like-minded leaders, the WEF ensures that its influence not only persists but also expands.

Yet, the power of the WEF isn't confined to soft influence alone. It exerts real, tangible pressure on nations and corporations to adopt its forward-thinking agendas. Through reports, rankings, and policy recommendations, it wields the stick and the carrot alike, guiding policy decisions in ways that often sideline local contexts and democratic deliberation. The term "stakeholder capitalism," widely promoted by the WEF, encapsulates this approach, prioritizing a governance model where unelected actors hold considerable sway over traditional, elected bodies.

A noteworthy aspect of the WEF's dominance is its ability to predict and set the agenda for global discourse. For instance, its early focus on the Fourth Industrial Revolution placed it at the forefront of conversations about artificial intelligence and automation long before these topics entered mainstream debate. By capitalizing on foresight, the WEF positions itself as a prophetic voice, one whose warnings and recommendations carry weight even before they're fully validated.

This influence is not without controversy. Critics argue that the WEF's initiatives often exacerbate existing inequalities and work primarily to safeguard elite interests. The focus on ESG (Environmental, Social, and Governance) criteria, widely endorsed by the WEF, exemplifies this tension. While ostensibly promoting sustainability and social responsibility, ESG frameworks can also serve as mechanisms for corporate control and economic gatekeeping, sidelining smaller players who can't afford to meet the stringent requirements.

The power of the WEF extends beyond businesses and policymakers; it shapes public opinion through media collaborations and extensive publication efforts. Reports, articles, and white papers curated by the WEF find their way into major media outlets, influencing narratives and framing issues in ways that align with its vision. This media strategy is instrumental in shaping a public consensus that aligns with the WEF's objectives, creating a feedback loop that reinforces its authority.

Nevertheless, it's important to recognize that the WEF doesn't operate in isolation. It collaborates closely with other influential entities such as the United Nations, International Monetary Fund, and World Bank, forming a complex web of alliances. These collaborations amplify its influence, enabling it to push for comprehensive policy changes that affect multiple layers of governance. The cross-pollination of ideas between these institutions creates a synergy that no single organization could achieve alone.

All this raises a crucial question: How does a body like the WEF reconcile its immense influence with the principles of democratic accountability? The organization's undemocratic nature—the fact that it wields power without direct electoral mandate—poses a legitimate concern. While it presents itself as a neutral platform for addressing global challenges, the WEF's underlying motivations and the ubiquity of its influence necessitate scrutiny.

In the end, the WEF's sway over global affairs is a testament to its strategic amalgamation of foresight, network, and narrative control. Its power is both pervasive and opaque, extending into spheres that affect our daily lives in ways that are often unperceived but profoundly impactful. Understanding the mechanisms through which the WEF operates is crucial for any critical examination of the 2030 agenda, as it remains a key driver behind many of the initiatives that this book seeks to explore and scrutinize.

Chapter 4:
The UN and Global Governance

The United Nations (UN) was established in 1945 with a mission to maintain international peace and security, develop friendly relations among nations, and promote social progress. Over the years, the UN has evolved into a massive organization with a broad range of responsibilities and a mix of successes and failures. Yet, as we look towards the future, specifically towards the 2030 Agenda, it seems the UN's role in global governance is taking on a more potent and, arguably, more ominous character.

The UN operates under the guise of fostering cooperation, but it's becoming increasingly clear that this cooperation comes at a significant cost. The centralization of authority and the push for a global standard often lead to individual nations sacrificing their sovereignty. On paper, the 2030 Agenda aims for sustainable development, equality, and the eradication of poverty. However, the methods proposed and the control required to achieve these goals raise serious concerns.

One of the most striking aspects of the UN's influence is its ability to delineate norms and practices that nations are encouraged, or sometimes compelled, to adopt. This top-down approach leaves little room for local context or national priorities. Under the banner of global governance, the UN has assumed a quasi-regulatory role that extends into various facets of life, from economic policies to social behaviors.

Through frameworks like the 2030 Agenda, the UN has reserved for itself the power to shape global actions. This document isn't merely a guideline; it's a detailed roadmap that sets specific targets for countries to achieve, often without accommodating differing regional realities. By tying these goals to funding and international support, the UN ensures compliance, sometimes at the expense of national autonomy.

Moreover, the UN's reach into global governance doesn't end at policy recommendations. Through its various specialized agencies, it exerts influence on healthcare, education, human rights, and environmental policies. Each of these areas comes with its own set of standards and expectations, pulling member states into alignment with a predefined global narrative that may not always align with domestic needs or values.

Take, for instance, the concept of sustainable development. While laudable in principle, in practice, it can compel countries to prioritize UN-defined sustainability goals over immediate domestic economic concerns. This can lead to friction, as nations struggle to balance the need for economic growth with the pressure to conform to global standards. The far-reaching consequences of such policies may undercut personal freedoms and economic opportunities, painting a rather dismal picture for those who value traditional notions of sovereignty.

Another troubling aspect is the lack of accountability within the UN framework. Decisions and policies can often be shaped by a handful of powerful member states, leaving smaller or developing nations with little say in the governance process. This inequity is particularly alarming when considering the extensive and sometimes intrusive nature of the 2030 Agenda.

In summary, the UN's role in global governance via the 2030 Agenda is multifaceted and powerful, but not without significant drawbacks. As this agenda unfolds, it's crucial to scrutinize the implications it has on national sovereignty, individual freedoms, and economic independence. The idea of a united world might sound appealing, but the reality is far more complex and, at times, unsettling.

Roles and Influence of the UN

The United Nations (UN) undoubtedly holds a pivotal place in the architecture of global governance. Founded in the aftermath of World War II, its establishment aimed to prevent future international conflicts and foster cooperation among nations. The UN's very foundation is rooted in the principles of peace, security, and human rights, which ostensibly positions it as a guardian of global stability. However, its influence has expanded far beyond these initial objectives, inserting itself into nearly every facet of global policy.

One of the most significant roles of the UN is its ability to set global agendas. Through various treaties, conventions, and initiatives, the UN has a knack for establishing far-reaching goals that member nations are expected to adopt. The 2030 Agenda for Sustainable Development is one such example, pushing comprehensive objectives that impact everything from energy policy to economic structuring. This agenda has been adopted by nearly all member states, thereby granting the UN a profound influence over national policies. But with this influence comes a disconcerting level of control that raises questions about sovereignty and autonomy.

The UN operates through multiple specialized agencies such as the World Health Organization (WHO), the International Monetary Fund (IMF), and the World Bank. These agencies provide expertise, financial aid, and policy recommendations that ostensibly aim to improve living standards globally. Yet, the economic strings attached to these aids often lead nations into politically motivated obligations. Countries that do not conform to the UN's stipulations might find themselves isolated or deprived of crucial support, displaying how the UN can wield soft power to enforce its visions.

Moreover, the UN's influence stretches into the realm of international law. Through the International Court of Justice (ICJ) and the International Criminal Court (ICC), the UN asserts judicial oversight over issues ranging from border disputes to alleged human rights violations. While these courts aim to deliver justice on a global scale, their jurisdiction and decision-making processes frequently spark debates about fairness and bias. Nations are sometimes caught between complying with international judgements and protecting their own legal sovereignty, a scenario that underscores the coercive potential hidden within the UN's noble missions.

The UN's influence further extends through its peacekeeping missions. Deployed to conflict zones around the world, UN peacekeepers are tasked with maintaining ceasefires and facilitating humanitarian aid. These missions are often seen as a last resort to mitigate violence, but they are not without criticism. Allegations of inefficacy and misconduct often surface, tarnishing the UN's reputation as an impartial peacekeeper. In some instances, the presence of UN peacekeepers can inadvertently entrench conflicts rather than resolve them, showcasing the limits of their capacity and oversight.

Additionally, the UN plays a crucial role in climate policy through conferences like the annual United Nations Climate Change Conference (COP). These gatherings are pivotal in formulating international climate agreements, such as the Kyoto Protocol and the Paris Agreement. By steering the discourse on environmental policies, the UN influences how nations address climate change, often pushing for drastic reforms that can significantly impact national industries and economies. While environmental sustainability is a vital goal, the ramifications on economic freedom and individual livelihoods can be substantial and evoke contentious debates.

Beyond its formal structures, the UN exerts an informal influence as a norm-setter in global ethics and practices. Issues such as gender equality, racial discrimination, and social inclusion are prominently featured in the UN's various campaigns and declarations. These initiatives shape international norms and encourage countries to adopt laws and policies aligned with what the UN deems as globally acceptable standards. Although such movements are framed within the language of human rights, they may conflict with cultural and social norms of diverse nations, instigating friction and resistance.

Critics often argue that the UN's overarching goals serve more to centralize global power rather than distribute it equitably. The intricate web of influence, seen in its myriad functions, suggests an organization with the capacity to shape, mold, and sometimes coerce nations into compliance. With this power, the UN can act as an enabler of an increasingly homogenized global order, potentially sidelining local voices and traditional governance structures. As we examine the role of the UN more critically, it is crucial to acknowledge both its capacity for positive global change and its potential for overreach and control.

Agenda 2030 and Its Global Impact

Agenda 2030, a blueprint put forth by the United Nations, stands as a complex and transformative policy that aims to reshape the world by addressing a myriad of social, economic, and environmental issues. However, beyond the facade of global improvement lies a subtle, yet potent, undercurrent of control that threatens to undermine individual freedoms and national sovereignty.

First, it's essential to understand what Agenda 2030 truly entails. Unveiled in 2015, the plan comprises 17 Sustainable Development Goals (SDGs) and 169 associated targets intended to transform our world by 2030. The SDGs range from eradicating poverty and hunger to achieving gender equality, promoting economic growth, and taking urgent action against climate change. While these goals are commendable on the surface, their implementation raises serious questions about global governance and the sacrifice of personal liberties for the sake of collectivism.

The implications of Agenda 2030 span across various dimensions of society. For one, the notion of sustainability is increasingly becoming a justification for governments to impose stringent regulations over private enterprises and individual choices. Industries, especially in manufacturing and agriculture, find themselves under unprecedented scrutiny, risking fines, and penalties if they do not comply with the rigid sustainability standards set forth by international bodies. In this scenario, the decision-making power is shifted from elected local governments to supranational entities, diluting electoral influence and accountability.

Furthermore, the emphasis on climate action often translates into heavy-handed policies that can have adverse economic impacts. In some cases, countries are pushed towards adopting green technologies and renewable energy resources without the infrastructure or financial capabilities to make the transition smoothly. This policy can inadvertently lead to economic instability, elevated energy prices, and job losses, disproportionately affecting low-income families who are more vulnerable to economic fluctuations.

Another sphere where Agenda 2030 exerts its influence is social policy. Goals such as gender equality and reduced inequalities are pursued with fervor, leading to extensive interventions in educational curriculums, workplace regulations, and social norms. While equality is a universally cherished principle, the methods for achieving it under Agenda 2030 often involve top-down mandates that stifle local traditions, cultural differences, and individual rights to freely associate or express oneself.

Concerns around privacy and personal data also come to the fore under Agenda 2030. The push for a digital economy and smart cities, with ubiquitous surveillance and data collection, heightens the risk of a surveillance state where individual actions are continuously monitored. Privacy, once considered a fundamental right, is increasingly being viewed as a trade-off for security and efficiency. This situation sets a dangerous precedent wherein data about individuals' lives and preferences are harvested, stored, and potentially exploited by both public and private sectors.

Economic models highlighted in Agenda 2030 lean towards centralized planning and control. The concept of "inclusive and sustainable economic growth" is laudable; however, its operationalization often implies higher taxes, increased government intervention, and redistribution of resources. These actions can stifle entrepreneurial spirit and innovation - two crucial engines of economic development. Small businesses and local enterprises find themselves competing on uneven playing fields dominated by corporations that are more equipped to comply with stringent global standards.

Internationally, Agenda 2030 positions the UN as a central figure in global governance. Countries are encouraged, and at times coerced, into aligning their national policies with the global agenda. The sovereignty of nations gets eroded as international norms and dictates find their way into domestic laws and regulations. This hierarchical governance model raises significant concerns about democracy and self-determination. Citizens face the conundrum of being subject to policies created thousands of miles away, often without their input or consent.

The interplay between Agenda 2030 and technological advancements cannot be ignored. The agenda promotes the utilization of technology to achieve its SDGs, but this also accelerates the march towards a technocratic governance system. Technology is not just a tool for development but becomes a means of control, surveillance, and enforcement. The pervasive role of Big Tech in collecting data, manipulating information flows, and shaping public opinion aligns seamlessly with the centralized planning ethos of Agenda 2030.

Critics argue that the cumulative impact of these policies points to a world where individual freedoms are curtailed in the name of collective good. The ostensibly noble goals of Agenda 2030 serve to mask an encroaching global governance structure that prioritizes control over autonomy, uniformity over diversity, and compliance over innovation.

Ultimately, the conversation around Agenda 2030 and its global impact is a nuanced one. While the intent to solve pressing global issues is apparent, the mechanisms deployed bring up significant ethical and practical dilemmas. The centralization of power, erosion of national sovereignty, and the trade-offs between security and freedom create a landscape where the future of personal liberties and democracy is fundamentally challenged.

In examining Agenda 2030, it is crucial to scrutinize not just the goals but the pathways chosen to achieve them. Mandatory compliance to vague, far-reaching mandates raises alarms about the loss of self-governance. Societies must critically assess how these sweeping changes imposed by global governance bodies align with the core principles of personal and economic freedoms. Only then can one truly understand the profound impact of Agenda 2030, far beyond its ostensibly benign objectives.

Chapter 5:
The Role of Canadian Politicians in the 2030 Agenda

As we delve into the intricate details of the 2030 Agenda, it's crucial to understand the role that Canadian politicians have played and continue to play in this global initiative. The ramifications of their involvement are far-reaching, shaping policies and influencing the daily lives of Canadian citizens. While the global goals of the 2030 Agenda are often wrapped in benevolent rhetoric, the local implementations can be quite different from the noble intentions set out initially.

At the forefront, key political figures in Canada have shown varied degrees of support for the 2030 Agenda. Individuals from different political parties have either championed its causes or raised concerns about its implications. Some view the agenda as a pathway to a more sustainable and equitable future, while others see it as a threat to national sovereignty and personal freedoms. For example, Justin Trudeau's administration has been a vocal supporter, pushing for policies aligned with the UN's Sustainable Development Goals (SDGs).

On the other hand, there's a growing faction of Canadian politicians who argue that the 2030 Agenda is an overreach by international bodies into domestic affairs. They cite potential risks to Canada's economic freedom and personal ownership. Conservative voices often highlight concerns about loss of autonomy and the imposition of policies that may not align with national interests or local needs. It's not just a question of sustainability but one of control and governance.

The policy implications of Canada's alignment with the 2030 Agenda are manifold. Environmental regulations, social justice initiatives, and economic reforms are just a few areas where the agenda's influence is felt. For instance, initiatives aimed at reducing carbon footprints have led to stringent regulations on industries, impacting everything from manufacturing to agriculture. These regulations, while intended to combat climate change, often come at a cost to small businesses and local economies.

Simultaneously, social initiatives driven by the 2030 Agenda focus on equity and inclusion. Policies promoting gender equality, reducing income inequality, and improving educational outcomes are essential components. These initiatives, while commendable in their goals, sometimes lead to contentious debates around implementation and effectiveness. The balance between achieving these goals and maintaining individual freedoms is a delicate one that Canadian politicians must navigate.

Moreover, the economic dimensions of the 2030 Agenda cannot be ignored. Efforts to shift towards a green economy, for example, have resulted in significant investments in renewable energy and sustainable technologies. However, this transition also bears the risk of economic displacement for workers in traditional energy sectors. The challenge for Canadian politicians is to manage these transitions in a way that minimizes negative impacts on the economy and employment.

Collaboration and conflict both characterize the role of Canadian politicians in the 2030 Agenda. On one hand, there's a need for international cooperation to address global challenges like climate change and social inequities. On the other hand, there's a need to protect national interests and sovereignty. This duality is a recurring theme in the political discourse around the 2030 Agenda in Canada.

As we move forward, the role of Canadian politicians will continue to evolve. The ongoing dialogue and debate around the 2030 Agenda will shape not just policy outcomes, but the very fabric of Canadian society. The stakes are high, and the decisions made today will resonate for generations to come. It's a complex and often contentious journey, but one that is crucial to understanding the broader implications of the 2030 Agenda.

Key Political Figures

In understanding the role of Canadian politicians in the 2030 Agenda, it's critical to recognize the key political figures who have played instrumental roles in shaping, supporting, and implementing these policies. Their influence and decisions set the tone for how Canada aligns with, and contributes to, this global initiative.

First and foremost, Prime Minister Justin Trudeau stands as a central figure in Canada's alignment with the 2030 Agenda. Since his election in 2015, Trudeau has consistently advocated for policies that align with the United Nations' Sustainable Development Goals (SDGs). His speeches at international summits and the policies he champions at home reflect a commitment to this agenda, often emphasizing environmental sustainability, social equity, and economic inclusivity. Trudeau's acceptance of global governance frameworks has significant implications for Canadian sovereignty, often placing international priorities at the forefront of national policy.

Alongside Trudeau, Chrystia Freeland, the Deputy Prime Minister and Minister of Finance, has also been a driving force behind Canada's economic policies that support the 2030 Agenda. Freeland's decisions around budget allocations and economic reforms frequently cite the need for equitable growth and sustainable development. Her leadership in navigating Canada's economy during challenging times, such as the COVID-19 pandemic, underscores her influence in steering the nation towards broader global goals.

Former Environment and Climate Change Minister Catherine McKenna played an essential role in aligning Canada's environmental policies with the 2030 Agenda. McKenna's tenure saw the introduction of significant climate policies including carbon pricing and investments in green technology. Her efforts were aimed at meeting Canada's commitments under the Paris Agreement, which is deeply connected to the 2030 Agenda's climate-related goals. McKenna's policies have had far-reaching impacts, both positive and controversial, in balancing economic impacts with environmental responsibilities.

Implicating the municipal level, mayors of major cities such as Toronto's John Tory and Vancouver's Kennedy Stewart also play crucial roles. These local leaders have integrated the 2030 Agenda into their urban planning and development policies. Issues like affordable housing, public transportation, and green spaces are addressed within the context of SDGs, aiming to create cities that meet global sustainability standards. Their local-level implementations feed into the broader national commitment to the 2030 Agenda.

Furthermore, Members of Parliament (MPs) from various parties contribute to the discourse around the 2030 Agenda. Notable among them are MPs like Elizabeth May from the Green Party, whose advocacy for stringent environmental protections directly aligns with SDGs. Conversely, some Conservative MPs, such as Pierre Poilievre, often critique the policies and question the implications for Canadian autonomy and economic freedom. This political dichotomy illustrates the contentious nature of the 2030 Agenda within the Canadian political landscape.

At the provincial level, premiers such as Alberta's Jason Kenney and Quebec's François Legault also have had their say in either promoting or resisting certain aspects of the 2030 Agenda. Kenney, for example, has often been vocal against federal policies that he perceives to undermine Alberta's oil and gas industry, arguing that such policies can detrimentally impact local economies. On the other hand, Legault's focus on sustainable energy, through hydropower projects, aligns more closely with Agenda 2030's environmentally-conscious goals.

In addition to elected officials, there are influential figures within the Canadian political sphere whose roles, while not necessarily front-and-center in the public eye, are critical. Bureaucrats and policy advisors, often operating within the Prime Minister's Office or specific ministries, help shape the strategies and frameworks that align with the 2030 Agenda. Their work behind the scenes ensures that Canada's policies are consistent with international commitments, often bridging gaps between political directives and practical implementations.

Moreover, non-political influencers like academics and think-tank leaders, such as those from the Canadian International Council (CIC) or the Conference Board of Canada, contribute to shaping public and governmental understanding of the 2030 Agenda. Their research, policy recommendations, and public engagements help contextualize international goals within the Canadian socio-economic environment, reinforcing—or at times challenging—the political narrative surrounding these initiatives.

Canada's role in the 2030 Agenda is not just a result of political leadership but also of political collaboration and, occasionally, confrontation. The convergence of different political perspectives results in a complex landscape where global commitments need to be balanced with national interests. The push and pull among various political figures create a dynamic environment, revealing the multifaceted nature of policy implementation and governance.

Understanding the contributions and opposition of these key political figures provides a clearer picture of how the 2030 Agenda is being assimilated within Canadian political frameworks. By examining their roles and actions, one can better appreciate the nuanced interplay of local priorities and global commitments, which ultimately shapes the country's path forward.

Policy Implications for Canada

The sweeping reforms outlined in the 2030 Agenda bring considerable policy implications for Canada. At its core, the agenda seeks to drastically reshape societal norms, requiring substantial adjustments and concerted efforts from Canadian politicians. This reformation period compels lawmakers to navigate a delicate balance between aligning with global objectives and safeguarding national interests.

One immediate consideration involves the realignment of Canada's legislative priorities. Politicians need to harmonize existing laws with the 2030 Agenda's vision, which might mean amending or even replacing cherished democratic principles. For instance, the Agenda's emphasis on environmental sustainability necessitates stringent environmental regulations, influencing sectors ranging from energy production to agriculture.

Economic policy is another significant facet influenced by the 2030 Agenda. With an eye on reducing inequality and promoting sustainable development, Canadian policymakers will face arduous choices. Redistribution of wealth and resources, critical elements of the Agenda, might entail higher taxes on corporations and the wealthy, potentially stifling entrepreneurial spirit. This raises questions about the balance between fostering economic growth and achieving equitable resource distribution.

Healthcare policy is set for a transformation too. The 2030 Agenda advocates for universal health coverage, which necessitates the reallocation of funds and possibly overhauling existing healthcare frameworks. Policymakers must develop strategies that ensure comprehensive coverage for all citizens, potentially increasing the burden on public finances. Simultaneously, integrating advancements in digital health technologies will be pivotal, raising additional concerns around data privacy and cyber security.

In the sphere of education, the 2030 Agenda champions equitable access to quality education. Canadian politicians are urged to elevate their efforts in reducing educational disparities. This necessitates increased funding for public schools, renewed focus on marginalized communities, and updates to the national curriculum to include sustainable development goals. How these policies will be funded amidst potential economic constraints remains a pressing issue.

Moreover, Canada's trade policies will also experience ramifications. The drive towards sustainable development may necessitate reviewing trade agreements to emphasize ethical labor practices and environmental stewardship. Canadian exporters could face new standards and regulations, affecting their competitive edge in the global market. Cautious refinement of trade policies will be essential to mitigate adverse economic impacts.

There's also the need to address digital transformation and privacy. The 2030 Agenda underscores the significance of leveraging digital technologies to achieve sustainable development. For Canada, this includes integrating smart technologies in various sectors and expanding digital infrastructures. Politicians must reconcile these advancements with robust data protection laws to safeguard citizens' privacy, a challenge in the era of rising cyber threats.

Indigenous rights and participation can't be overlooked. The 2030 Agenda stresses leaving no one behind, pressing Canadian politicians to enhance efforts towards reconciliation and inclusive development. Policymakers must ensure that Indigenous communities not only benefit from sustainable development policies but also play an integral role in policy formulation and implementation. This approach demands enhanced dialogue, trust-building, and perhaps reparative initiatives.

Climate policy will inevitably come under scrutiny as well. Canada, known for its natural resources, particularly in oil and gas, will need to navigate transitional policies towards renewable energy sources. This could entail introducing stringent emission reduction targets, incentivizing green technologies, and phasing out fossil fuel dependence. These actions, while essential, may face resistance from industry stakeholders and certain provincial governments.

Social policies, specifically those targeting poverty reduction and social equity, will align more closely with the 2030 Agenda's goals. Legislators will need to spearhead initiatives tailored to eradicating poverty, reducing social inequalities, and fostering inclusive socioeconomic growth. Programs supporting affordable housing, enhancing social safety nets, and improving access to essential services will become focal points of legislative action.

Furthermore, the Agenda's robust call for gender equality demands amplified policy attention. Canadian politicians must ensure effective implementation of gender-responsive policies across all sectors. This includes enforcing equal pay legislations, bolstering support for women in leadership roles, and addressing gender-based violence. Achieving genuine gender equality will mean transcending token gestures towards structural changes.

Lastly, international collaboration and commitment are cornerstone elements. Canadian politicians will need to fortify alliances with other nations pursuing the 2030 Agenda. This fosters a transnational sharing of strategies and aligning efforts towards global sustainability. However, harmonizing national interests with international commitments will be a nuanced dance, requiring diplomatic finesse and strategic priority-setting.

In summary, the policy implications for Canada within the framework of the 2030 Agenda are profound and multifaceted. Canadian politicians are tasked with a daunting yet critical role: to usher in reforms that are not only beneficial on a global scale but also serve the nation's best interests. This transformative journey demands astute governance, resilient policies, and an unwavering commitment to balancing global objectives with preserving national integrity.

Chapter 6:
Digital ID and Privacy Concerns

Digital IDs are essentially electronic versions of identity documents like passports and national ID cards. They're designed to provide a streamlined, unified way to verify identity across various services, both public and private. While digital IDs promise convenience, efficiency, and even enhanced security, they come with significant privacy concerns.

A key issue with digital IDs is the centralization of personal data. When all of your information is stored in one place, it becomes a valuable target for hackers. The risk of massive data breaches increases exponentially, and the consequences could be devastating. Imagine your entire identity, from medical records to financial information, being compromised in an instant.

Moreover, digital IDs could potentially allow governments and corporations unprecedented access to personal data. The concept of privacy becomes blurry when so much of your behavior can be tracked and analyzed. Shopping habits, travel routes, and even social interactions might be logged, enabling a level of surveillance that was previously unimaginable.

There's also the fear of misuse by the authorities. History has shown that increased surveillance powers often come at the expense of civil liberties. Digital IDs could easily be weaponized to silence dissent or discriminate against certain groups. The balance between security and freedom is delicate, and tipping the scales too far in favor of surveillance could have dire ramifications.

In many cases, the implementation of digital IDs lacks transparency. Citizens are rarely involved in the decision-making process, and concerns are often dismissed as paranoia or conspiracy theories. This lack of dialogue exacerbates the mistrust between the public and those in power. Open discussions about the pros and cons of digital IDs are essential for crafting policies that protect individual freedoms.

Finally, we must consider the ethical implications. Who controls the data? Who has access to it? These questions are crucial in a world where data is arguably more valuable than oil. Ensuring that digital IDs do not become tools of oppression or unnecessary intrusion is vital for preserving personal privacy and autonomy.

What Digital ID Entails

Digital ID represents a complex and multifaceted system designed to provide individuals with a verifiable and standardized form of identification in the digital world. At its core, a digital identity is a compilation of an individual's attributes and identifiers that have been digitized to enable authentication and authorization. This can include biometrics like fingerprints or facial recognition, digital certificates, and other forms of electronic identification. The implementation of such a system is not just about replacing traditional IDs but aims to integrate various aspects of a person's life into a single digital profile.

One of the key arguments in favor of digital IDs is their potential to streamline services and enhance convenience. For example, with a robust digital ID infrastructure, citizens could access government services, healthcare, and financial services with minimal friction. Imagine renewing a driver's license or filing taxes online securely without the need to appear in person or submit physical documents.

Proponents argue that this consolidation can lead to significant administrative efficiencies and reduce costs for both individuals and institutions.

However, the ubiquity of digital ID systems opens a Pandora's box of privacy concerns. The consolidation of personal data into a singular digital profile creates a valuable target for cybercriminals and hackers. The potential for data breaches becomes exponentially higher when centralized databases hold vast amounts of sensitive information. It's a double-edged sword; while centralization can lead to streamlined processes, it also means a single point of failure could expose vast amounts of personal data.

The interoperability of digital IDs across various platforms and services is another aspect to consider. The goal is to create a universally applicable ID that can be used for multiple purposes across both the public and private sectors. While this can facilitate easier access to services, it also raises questions about data sharing and the boundaries of surveillance. Who controls this data? Who gets access? And, most importantly, how can individuals safeguard their digital identities against misuse?

Digital identity systems also require robust infrastructures that can ensure the security and integrity of the data. This necessitates significant investments in technology, cybersecurity measures, and regulatory frameworks. Blockchain technology often comes up in discussions about secure digital ID implementations, but it's not without its own set of challenges and limitations. The decentralized, immutable nature of blockchain does offer some security advantages but integrating it into existing systems poses unique hurdles and complexities.

In some instances, digital IDs could also exacerbate existing inequalities. Not everyone has the same level of access to digital technologies, and disparities in digital literacy can make adoption uneven. Marginalized communities might find themselves further excluded if digital ID systems become the norm without inclusive measures to ensure universal accessibility. The concept of a digital divide thus becomes even more pressing in the context of digital identification.

The international move toward digital IDs is also driven by globalization and the need for standardized identification systems for cross-border transactions and interactions. For instance, the European Union's eIDAS regulation aims to facilitate secure electronic transactions across member states, setting a precedent for what a global digital ID could look like. But this raises complications, especially in terms of data sovereignty and jurisdictional control over personal information, complicating the already intricate web of international laws and frameworks.

Digital ID systems can fundamentally alter the relationship between the state and its citizens. The implications are vast, especially when considering the power dynamics involved. Imagine a world where access to essential services could be contingent on a government-issued digital ID. This centralization of power could easily be misused, leading to an erosion of civil liberties and increased state control over individual lives. This brings to mind various dystopian scenarios where the state has unprecedented surveillance capabilities and control over its citizens.

Moreover, the integration of artificial intelligence and machine learning into digital ID systems is gradually becoming a reality. These technologies can enhance the capabilities of digital IDs, providing real-time verification and more sophisticated forms of authentication. However, they also introduce new risks, such as algorithmic biases and lack of transparency in decision-making processes. These issues must be addressed to prevent the perpetuation of inequalities and unjust practices.

As digital IDs become more entrenched in daily life, the importance of legal and ethical frameworks will only grow. Regulations need to be put in place to protect individuals' rights and ensure that the systems are used responsibly. This involves creating stringent guidelines around data protection, user consent, and accountability for breaches or misuse. Transparency in how the systems operate and how data is managed is crucial for public trust and acceptance.

Ultimately, while the promise of digital IDs is alluring, the intricate weaving of personal data into a singular digital tapestry carries enormous risks. As we fast approach the implementation of such systems under the aegis of agendas like the 2030 Agenda, it is crucial to be scrupulous about the accompanying privacy concerns. Only through vigilant regulation, robust technological safeguards, and inclusive policies can the potential of digital IDs be harnessed while mitigating its inherent risks.

Invasion of Privacy: Risks and Ramifications

The rise of digital IDs poses a significant threat to personal privacy, raising concerns that transcend simple data collection. Digital IDs, while marketed as modern conveniences and tools for better governance, come with a host of risks. The first and most glaring is the erosion of individual privacy. Once personal information is stored digitally, it becomes vulnerable to unauthorized access, misuse, and surveillance.

Imagine a world where every action you take is monitored, recorded, and potentially used against you. This is not a dystopian fantasy; it's a potential reality with comprehensive digital ID systems. Governments and corporations alike could gain unprecedented insight into our lives. Every transaction, movement, and even social interaction could be tracked. It's a stark invasion of what used to be considered sacrosanct personal space.

Besides the existential threat to privacy, there are concrete ramifications for individuals. The centralization of personal data in digital IDs could facilitate identity theft on an unprecedented scale. Hackers could potentially access extensive datasets, leading to financial loss and personal distress. As data breaches become more common, the damages could span years, or even decades, affect victims across their personal and professional lives.

The ramifications extend beyond personal consequences. When authorities have access to detailed information about citizens, the potential for abuse looms large. Consider a scenario where political dissent or undesirable behavior is punished through subtle means like denial of services or suspension of digital IDs. The lack of transparency about how data is used or who has access to it only exacerbates these concerns. Authoritarian regimes could exploit these systems to maintain power and control, stifling freedom of speech and democracy itself.

Add to this the complication of data sharing agreements between governments and corporations. Many digital ID systems are implemented in partnership with private firms, which ostensibly hold the same data security standards. However, the profit motive could lead to data being sold to the highest bidder. Corporations could use this data for targeted advertising, creating profiles of users that include their habits, preferences, and vulnerabilities. This commodification of personal data turns individuals into products.

The risks are not confined to bad actors alone. Even well-meaning data collection and analysis can lead to unintended consequences. Algorithms, no matter how sophisticated, are designed and programmed by humans. They are prone to biases which can lead to discriminatory practices. For instance, predictive policing algorithms might target minority communities disproportionately, cultivating systemic discrimination under the guise of data-driven decisions.

Moreover, the psychological impact of constant surveillance cannot be understated. Knowing that one's actions are continually being watched generates a culture of fear and compliance. People might alter their behavior, censor their speech, and withdraw from public discourse to avoid potential repercussions. When privacy is compromised, the fundamental right to express oneself freely is also jeopardized, leading to a more conformist and less vibrant society.

It's also important to consider the geopolitical ramifications. Countries that adopt expansive digital ID systems may pressure others to follow suit, claiming benefits like enhanced security and streamlined administration. This trend towards uniformity could lead to a global loss of privacy. The interplay of international politics may also result in cross-border data sharing agreements, further complicating personal data protection.

And there's the matter of digital exclusion. Not all individuals have equal access to technology, and reliance on digital IDs could marginalize those without the necessary resources or skills. Elderly persons, the economically disadvantaged, and rural populations may find it difficult to navigate increasingly digitized systems, adding to their isolation and disenfranchisement.

Some may argue that these risks are outweighed by the benefits of digital IDs in combating fraud, improving administrative efficiency, and providing seamless access to services. While these benefits are tangible, they should not come at the cost of personal freedom and security. It's crucial to scrutinize and restrict the extent of data collected, and to enforce stringent safeguards to prevent misuse.

In conclusion, the implementation of digital IDs harbors numerous risks that could drastically infringe on personal privacy. The ramifications are multifaceted, affecting individuals, society, and international relations. As we inch closer to a future dominated by digital identification, it is imperative to weigh these risks judiciously, ensuring that the preservation of privacy remains a cardinal priority. Without rigorous checks and balances, the convenience digital IDs promise may come at far too great a cost.

Chapter 7:
Government Control Over Finance

The structure of modern financial systems underscores a critical relationship between governments and financial autonomy. Today, the notion that individuals can freely manage their finances without governmental interference is increasingly becoming a myth. To understand this shift, we need to delve into how governments leverage financial systems to assert control and limit freedoms. Historically, finance has been the lifeblood of autonomy, a means for individuals and businesses to thrive independently. However, the trajectory is changing rapidly.

Governments have employed a variety of methods to gain control over financial systems. Central banks play a pivotal role in this endeavor. By managing currency issuance and interest rates, they have an extraordinary ability to influence economies. Through mechanisms such as quantitative easing and fiscal policies, central banks can manipulate economic conditions, subtly pulling strings that guide the financial behavior of the populace. These actions are often justified as necessary for economic stability and growth, but rarely do they emphasize the trade-offs involved, such as reduced financial freedom.

Moreover, the increased use of financial regulations and monitoring systems has further tightened governmental grip. Anti-money laundering (AML) measures, while ostensibly targeting crime, grant governments the power to scrutinize individual movements and financial transactions. The Financial Action Task Force (FATF) and similar bodies are instruments that global governance entities use to standardize these controls across nations. Compliance requires banks and financial institutions to share extensive customer data, leaving individuals with little to no privacy in their financial dealings.

Financial surveillance isn't just about monitoring; it's about control. Governments often leverage this surveillance to suppress dissent and promote conformity. By tracking and potentially freezing assets, they can stifle political opposition or activism. These tactics are not theoretical—numerous instances exist where banks have frozen the accounts of activists or political adversaries, effectively neutralizing movements by cutting off their financial lifelines.

Then there's the concept of de-banking, an increasingly prevalent form of financial exclusion. This occurs when individuals or organizations are denied access to banking services due to their political views, associations, or behavior deemed non-compliant with regulatory expectations. It epitomizes how financial control can serve as a tool for broader societal regulation.

Digital finance has further accelerated the potential for government control. Cryptocurrencies initially promised a decentralized financial future, free from government intervention. However, regulations are catching up fast. Governments are designing laws to monitor and control these digital assets, often citing concerns over fraud and money laundering as rationales. The very anonymity and decentralization that gave cryptocurrencies their appeal are now under threat.

Of course, government intervention in finance is not solely about control. From their perspective, it's about maintaining systemic stability, preventing crises, and thwarting illegal activities. But such motivations cloud the underlying cost—the erosion of personal financial freedom. Every regulation, every surveillance measure, tightens the grip around the narrative that the state knows best how to manage financial behaviors.

As we navigate this landscape, it becomes clear that understanding financial control mechanisms is crucial for preserving individual autonomy. While the rationale behind governmental influence can indeed have merit, the implications for personal freedom cannot be ignored. The 2030 Agenda encompasses these dynamics, envisioning a future where enhanced governmental oversight becomes an unwavering norm.

In this intricate web of policies and regulations, financial freedom teeters on a delicate balance. The need for vigilance, awareness, and proactive resistance to encroachments on autonomy cannot be overstated. As you assess the broader impact of governmental control over financial systems, consider the profound implications for both individual freedoms and societal structures.

Financial Systems and Freedoms

As we delve deeper into the mechanics of the 2030 Agenda, it's crucial to grasp the profound impact it has on financial systems and personal freedoms. The goal of creating an equitable society, as championed by global organizations, often translates into a substantial increase in governmental control over financial transactions. This chapter will examine the intersection of finance and freedom, highlighting the inherent risks and subtle mechanisms of control that can stifle individual liberties.

Traditionally, financial systems have enabled freedom by allowing individuals to buy, sell, trade, and save in whatever manner suits them best. This freedom, however, is increasingly challenged by policies that facilitate more stringent oversight and regulation. The rhetoric often suggests that such measures are necessary for security and economic stability. Nonetheless, these justifications frequently mask a more insidious encroachment on personal economic autonomy.

From credit scoring systems to anti-money laundering laws, the extent to which governments monitor and influence financial behavior is expanding. On the surface, these initiatives aim to tackle crime and ensure tax compliance. However, deeper inspection reveals a growing infrastructure that allows for unprecedented scrutiny of everyday transactions. The balance between legitimate oversight and overreach is perilously delicate.

One significant shift is the rising prominence of cashless societies. While the convenience and efficiency of digital payments are undeniable, they come with a critical trade-off. Every digital transaction leaves a trace, creating a comprehensive record that can be analyzed, stored, and potentially exploited. As cash becomes less common, the anonymity it offers in financial dealings is diminishing, placing ever more power in the hands of those who control the data.

Moreover, the introduction of digital identities linked to financial systems takes surveillance to another level. When financial activities are tied to a centralized digital ID, it becomes exponentially easier for authorities to track and analyze behavior. As a result, the potential for misuse, whether for political targeting or other unseemly purposes, grows correspondingly.

Financial freedoms are also threatened by initiatives that promote universal basic income (UBI). Though often painted as a benevolent policy aimed at eradicating poverty, UBI can come with strings attached. Dependence on a government-provided income can erode personal initiative and entrepreneurship, leading to a populace that's more pliant and easier to control. Furthermore, the power to distribute or withhold financial resources can become a tool for enforcing conformity and compliance with governmental edicts.

Additionally, measures such as negative interest rates and bail-ins serve as tools for controlling monetary flow. These methods, applied under the guise of economic stabilization, effectively coerce individuals into specific financial behaviors, whether it's discouraging saving via negative interest rates or absorbing individual savings during bank bail-ins to stabilize financial institutions. The underlying message is clear: personal financial autonomy must take a backseat to the perceived needs of the larger economic system.

The creation and enforcement of stringent tax regulations also play a big role in curbing financial freedom. Stricter policies on reporting and compliance not only impact large corporations and the wealthy but also trickle down to small businesses and individuals. The cost of compliance and the fear of punitive measures often deter entrepreneurial ventures, stifling innovation and economic growth.

The attainments of various financial systems often mask the omnipresence of governmental influence. Regulations and oversight are packaged to seem benign or even beneficial. However, when scrutinized closely, it becomes evident that these systems are designed to consolidate control over financial mobility and independence. A controlled financial environment makes it easier for governments to monitor, influence, and, if necessary, restrict the financial behaviors of individuals.

Also noteworthy is the evolution of credit systems that now factor in behavioral analytics and social behavior indicators. Though initially intended to gauge creditworthiness, these systems can easily transition into mechanisms for social control. For instance, an individual's financial opportunities may become contingent on behaviors deemed acceptable by the state, effectively creating a socio-economic loop that rewards compliance and punishes deviation.

The danger lies not only in the current applications of these systems but also in their potential future uses. The frameworks being established today enable a degree of financial control that could be exploited for more oppressive purposes down the line. Vigilance and discernment are essential in understanding these developments and advocating for policies that prioritize genuine financial freedoms over superficial protections.

For a concrete example, consider the dangers exemplified by China's social credit system (discussed in another chapter). What may start as financial regulation can evolve into a broader framework of control affecting many aspects of life. The specter of such systems should be a stark warning against the uncritical acceptance of increasing governmental control over finance.

The gradual erosion of financial freedoms under the guise of regulation and security is a key element of the 2030 Agenda's broader aims. As we move forward, understanding these changes and their implications becomes not just an academic exercise but a necessary step for safeguarding individual liberties. The intersection of financial systems and personal freedoms is thus not just a topic of economic policy but a battleground for the very essence of personal autonomy and independence.

How Governments Gain Control

Governments, by virtue of their structure and need to maintain order, have always had a vested interest in exerting control over various aspects of society, and finance is no exception. Financial systems are the backbone of any economy, influencing everything from national policy to everyday commerce. By gaining control over financial systems, governments can exert a high degree of influence over their citizens' lives, often under the guise of stability and security. This control manifests in various ways, affecting both macroeconomic conditions and individual financial freedoms.

One prominent method through which governments assert control is via central banks and monetary policy. Central banks, often portrayed as independent entities, are frequently influenced by governmental priorities. By adjusting interest rates, setting reserve requirements, and engaging in open market operations, these banks have the power to steer economic activity. The ability to control inflation and currency stability is powerful, but it can also be used to manipulate economic conditions to serve specific political objectives.

Another tool at governments' disposal is regulation. Financial regulations are ostensibly designed to protect consumers and ensure market stability, yet they often serve broader agendas. Consider the plethora of compliance requirements for banks and financial institutions. While these regulations aim to prevent malfeasance and protect the financial system, they also create mechanisms for monitoring and controlling economic activities. Regulatory frameworks can be tightened or loosened to reward or penalize certain behaviors, effectively swaying market dynamics and influencing business decisions.

Taxation is another critical lever. By instituting various forms of taxes—income, corporate, capital gains—governments generate revenue while also influencing economic behavior. High taxes on certain sectors can disincentivize investment in those areas, while tax breaks on others can spur growth. The power to tax is the power to destroy or foster particular industries and behaviors, offering governments an often-overlooked avenue for exerting control.

Innovation in financial technology has also provided governments with new means of control. Digital currencies and blockchain technology were initially envisioned as decentralized alternatives to traditional financial systems. However, governments have swiftly moved to incorporate these technologies into their existing frameworks. Central Bank Digital Currencies (CBDCs) are a prime example. By developing their own digital currencies, governments gain unprecedented tracking and regulatory capabilities. Every transaction made with a CBDC can be monitored, offering granular insights into economic behavior. This isn't just about oversight—it's about the potential to influence how money is spent, saved, and invested.

Sanctions and international finance provide yet another avenue for control. Governments can exert influence beyond their borders by leveraging financial systems. Sanctions, whether targeting individuals, companies, or entire nations, are a powerful tool for enforcing international norms and punishing perceived misbehavior. The ability to restrict access to global financial networks can cripple economies and force compliance with international agendas. The SWIFT network, for instance, is an integral part of global finance, and being cut off from it can have devastating consequences.

In times of crisis, the degree of control tends to expand. Economic downturns, wars, and pandemics have all prompted governments to take more substantial control over financial systems. Emergency measures—sometimes temporary, sometimes not—expand the scope of governmental intervention. Stimulus packages, bailouts, and economic relief programs are all means by which the government can direct resources, influence markets, and ensure adherence to specific policy goals.

Subsidies and incentives can also not be overlooked. By providing subsidies to favored industries or offering incentives for particular investments, governments can shape the economic landscape according to their strategic objectives. These financial mechanisms can prop up certain sectors while letting others languish, guiding economic development in prescribed directions.

The question of transparency and accountability in these methods of control is crucial. While some level of oversight and regulation is necessary for the stability and security of financial systems, the concentration of power can be problematic. Transparency is often lacking, and the checks and balances designed to prevent abuse can be insufficient. The potential for overreach is ever-present, and it's a delicate balance between facilitating economic stability and infringing on individual freedoms.

Financial surveillance has also evolved significantly. Know Your Customer (KYC) and Anti-Money Laundering (AML) regulations require extensive information gathering and monitoring of financial transactions. While these measures aim to prevent illegal activities, they also provide governments with detailed insights into personal financial behaviors. The capability to monitor and analyze these data points can be both a protective measure and a means of control.

Finally, there's the matter of public acceptance and resistance. People may support some forms of financial control for the perceived benefits of security and stability. However, excessive control can lead to pushback, dissent, and calls for greater financial autonomy. Understanding this dynamic is crucial for any government attempting to assert control without inciting public unrest.

As governments continue to navigate the complexities of modern finance, the balance between control and freedom remains a central issue. The tools at their disposal are potent and varied, and the implications for personal and economic freedom are profound. Vigilance and informed discourse are essential to ensuring that these powers are used judiciously and in the public interest.

Chapter 8:
Central Bank Digital Currencies: Control Mechanisms

Central Bank Digital Currencies (CBDCs) represent a seismic shift in the realm of finance and monetary policy. These state-backed digital currencies are designed to provide a digital equivalent of paper money, but their implications run much deeper than a mere shift to digital forms. The overarching concern here is the potential for unprecedented government control over individual financial transactions and, by extension, personal freedoms.

CBDCs allow central banks to have real-time data on all transactions—something cash never did. This level of visibility can be used to monitor, control, and even restrict how money is spent. Imagine a scenario where the government can limit your purchases based on policy goals or social planning objectives. The possibilities for misuse are alarming. This intrusiveness is not a dystopian fantasy but a plausible outcome when powers centralize digital financial data.

Another chilling aspect is programmability. CBDCs can be designed to expire if not used by a certain date, or restricted to specific uses. Governments could dictate that your digital currency must be spent on "green" products or forfeited. Such mechanisms can erode economic freedom and individual autonomy. This potent tool can enforce behavioral changes en masse, something previously infeasible with physical currencies.

Financial privacy is another casualty in the adoption of CBDCs. Every transaction recorded and monitored creates a detailed profile of spending habits, habits which could easily be misused by those in power. Traditional banking systems and cash transactions at least provided some semblance of privacy. The stakes here are much higher, with potential ramifications reaching far beyond financial data.

Furthermore, the control mechanisms embedded in CBDCs could serve as a gateway to broader social credit systems, integrating financial data with other personal data to create comprehensive citizen profiles. These profiles could then be used to reward or punish behaviors, all under the veneer of legal and economic management.

Given these concerns, many argue that the introduction of CBDCs should be halted entirely. The risk of spiraling into a surveillance state with heavy-handed fiscal control is too dire to ignore. It is not merely a question of convenience or innovation, but one of preserving personal freedoms and rights in a rapidly evolving digital age.

Introduction to CBDCs

Central Bank Digital Currencies (CBDCs) open a new chapter in the realm of monetary control and governance. At their core, CBDCs are digital renditions of a country's fiat currency, issued and regulated by the nation's central bank. Unlike cryptocurrencies such as Bitcoin, which are decentralized and operate outside government control, CBDCs are state-controlled digital assets. Their primary promise is to modernize the financial landscape by creating a more efficient, inclusive, and transparent monetary system. However, the journey towards implementing CBDCs brings forth a plethora of control mechanisms that could significantly alter how individuals interact with their money and their government.

The concept of control is deeply embedded in the architecture of CBDCs. One of the primary mechanisms through which CBDCs exercise control is programmability. Picture this: governments could impose conditions on how and when the digital currency can be used. For example, money could be programmed to expire if not spent within a certain time frame, or it could be restricted to specific types of transactions. This introduces an unprecedented granular level of financial surveillance and control that could undermine personal financial sovereignty.

Another aspect to consider is the potential for negative interest rates. In a scenario where traditional cash is replaced by a central bank's digital currency, the central authority could impose negative interest rates on holdings. This is aimed at stimulating economic activity, encouraging spending over saving. But it also means that individuals could lose money simply by holding onto it, a concept that breaks from the traditional store of value principle.

While proponents argue that CBDCs could reduce instances of money laundering and tax evasion, the trade-off comes at a cost to privacy. Every transaction made with a CBDC is likely to be recorded and monitored, giving central authorities unprecedented insight into individuals' spending habits. This brings about significant concerns on the boundaries between security measures and individual freedoms.

The transition from physical cash to digital currency can also lead to greater economic inclusivity, providing the unbanked population with access to financial services. However, it is essential to question whether this inclusivity might come with strings attached. For instance, digital inclusion could become a tool for mass surveillance and behavioral control.

Moreover, CBDCs can traverse national boundaries more fluidly than traditional fiat currencies. While this might simplify international transactions and reduce costs, it also opens Pandora's box for geopolitical leverage. Countries could use their digital currency as a means of exerting influence over others, potentially causing more friction in an already complex global financial landscape.

When integrated with a national identity system, CBDCs could serve as a vital component of a broader digital infrastructure. This amalgamation would tie individual identity specifics with financial transactions, integrating various layers of personal data. The efficiency gains from such a system could be considerable, but it poses daunting questions about privacy invasion and centralization of control.

The allure of CBDCs also lies in their potential flexibility in monetary policy implementation. Central banks could rapidly adjust supply and transaction conditions in response to economic shifts. However, this kind of adaptability might also give rise to overreach and arbitrary measures, disrupting market stability and individual trust in the monetary system.

Finally, the narrative around financial inclusion and technological innovation often overshadows the discourse on control mechanisms. It is crucial to strike a balance between leveraging the benefits of digital currencies and safeguarding liberties. Critical examination and public discourse are essential in ensuring that the implementation of CBDCs doesn't compromise freedoms under the guise of innovation.

As we delve deeper into the control mechanisms of CBDCs, it becomes clear that behind their benefits, substantial risks to economic freedom and privacy loom. Understanding these implications is vital as we navigate through the digital age, shaping a future that doesn't forsake our core values for technological convenience.

Why They Should Be Stopped

Central Bank Digital Currencies (CBDCs) present a far-reaching shift in how monetary systems operate, ostensibly designed for enhanced efficiency and security. Beneath the surface, however, lie troubling implications for personal freedom and financial autonomy. As the digitization of global currencies becomes more imminent, a stark realization emerges: surrendering unchecked control to central banks invites a cascade of risks that should prompt serious reconsideration.

One of the primary concerns about CBDCs is the unprecedented level of surveillance they enable. Traditional cash transactions allow for a degree of privacy—something that digital currencies overseen by central banks obliterate. Every transaction, from buying a coffee to funding a political group, can be monitored, recorded, and potentially scrutinized. It's not just about privacy; it's about the ability for institutions to overreach, undermining personal liberty under the guise of financial regulation.

This all-encompassing surveillance opens the door to a new form of financial censorship. Imagine a scenario where the central authority deems certain expenditures undesirable or non-compliant with societal values. The bureaucrats in charge could freeze assets, restrict purchases, or impose penalties—not based on legality, but based on subjective moral judgments or political motivations. This transformation of money into a tool of control harkens back to dystopian narratives of totalitarian regimes, yet it's no longer a theoretical exercise—it's a looming reality.

The centralization of financial power into the hands of a few also undermines economic diversity and resilience. Decentralized systems, such as those offered by traditional cash and emerging cryptocurrencies, create robust networks where power is distributed. CBDCs, however, funnel control into the central banks, making economic systems more susceptible to failures, mismanagement, or even rogue governance. Should a singular entity err or act out of self-interest, the cascading effects could devastate entire economies, leaving citizens powerless.

Moreover, the introduction of programmable money within CBDCs sets a dangerous precedent. Imagine a central authority defining not just how much money you have, but how you can spend it. Funds could be programmed to expire if not used within a set period. Financial assistance could come with strings attached, limiting spending to 'approved' vendors or prohibiting savings altogether. These measures strip away financial autonomy, morphing citizens into mere operators within a controlled economic machine.

CBDCs also pose a threat to civic freedoms through the potential for social credit-style systems. By linking financial transactions with social metrics, authorities can reward or penalize behavior, effectively enforcing conformity through economic pressure. The precedents set in countries like China, where social credit systems already dictate aspects of daily life, should serve as a cautionary tale. There's a fine line between incentives and coercion, and CBDCs make crossing that line simpler.

Concerns about security and hacking are often raised with digital systems but here, they resonate even louder. A centralized digital currency system becomes a tantalizing target for cybercriminals. A single breach could jeopardize the financial data and assets of millions, if not billions, of people. The historical precedents of data breaches that have occurred even in the most secure environments underscore the inherent risks associated with concentrating so much sensitive information.

In addition to security concerns, the implementation of CBDCs necessitates immense investments in technological infrastructure. The argument for the 'greater good' is frequently invoked to justify these expenses, but this often translates into taxpayer burdens. Resources that could be better spent on public services, healthcare, education, and infrastructure are diverted into an intricate and overarching financial control system which may offer minimal benefits in comparison to its costs and risks.

From a geopolitical perspective, adopting CBDCs may also elevate risks of economic warfare. Countries with more developed digital currencies could theoretically exert influence over those still dependent on traditional or semi-digital systems. The balance of economic power can shift, allowing dominant economies to dictate terms and engage in economic coercion. This indirect form of imperialism, underpinned by financial dominance, could destabilize global markets and exacerbate inequalities.

Additionally, it is worth highlighting that the imposition of CBDCs can marginalize underbanked populations. While proponents argue that digital currencies can enhance financial inclusion, the opposite can also be true. Those without access to digital devices, stable internet, or the requisite technological literacy may find themselves further excluded. The digital divide, often accentuated by socio-economic disparities, could widen as a result, thus defeating one of the purported objectives of CBDCs.

The ethical considerations cannot be ignored either. Trust between governments and citizens is foundational to a functioning society. The implementation of CBDCs, perceived or real, enhances surveillance, control, and economic manipulation. This erosion of trust could engender public resistance, civil unrest, and a potential breakdown in the social contract. Governments should be wary of these long-lasting implications and tread cautiously.

In conclusion, as promising as Central Bank Digital Currencies may appear on the surface, their extensive control mechanisms suggest a foreboding trajectory. Surveillance, censorship, centralization, and susceptibility to misuse make them a perilous gamble. It's critical that these ramifications are thoroughly considered and debated before taking steps that could irrevocably alter the financial landscape and societal freedoms. These cautionary reasons collectively form a compelling case for why CBDCs should be halted at least until there's a clear, democratic, and secure way forward. The risks are too significant, and the stakes too high, to proceed without stringent scrutiny and robust safeguards.

Chapter 9:
Leading Countries in Central Bank Digital Currency Initiatives

In a rapidly digitizing world, Central Bank Digital Currencies (CBDCs) have emerged as a potent tool for financial regulation and control. Several nations are spearheading the development and implementation of CBDCs, marking a significant shift in how governments manage currency and economic oversight. These initiatives present both opportunities and challenges, particularly in the context of the 2030 Agenda and the broader implications of such financial innovations.

China is arguably the forerunner in the CBDC race. The People's Bank of China (PBOC) has been actively developing the Digital Currency Electronic Payment (DCEP), commonly referred to as the digital yuan. Testing began in major cities with plans to extend its use nationwide. China's push for a digital currency can be seen as part of a broader strategy to strengthen government control over the financial system, enhance surveillance capabilities, and diminish the influence of cryptocurrencies that operate outside of government purview.

The European Central Bank (ECB) is not far behind with its digital euro project. Though still in the investigative phase, the ECB has underscored the importance of a digital euro to ensure the sovereignty of its monetary system amidst growing digitalization. The initiative aims to safeguard public trust in the European currency while addressing challenges posed by other global digital currencies and private digital payment systems. The ECB's approach remains cautious, focusing on thoroughly assessing the potential impacts on the banking sector, monetary policy, and overall financial stability.

Sweden stands out in the European landscape with its advanced exploration of the e-krona. The Sveriges Riksbank has been conducting pilot programs for a few years, driven by a substantial decline in the use of cash. The e-krona initiative aims to ensure that the public continues to have access to state-backed money while adapting to a largely digital economy. Like other CBDC projects, the e-krona raises questions about privacy, financial inclusion, and the role of banks in distributing digital currency.

In the Caribbean, the Bahamas has made remarkable strides with the launch of the Sand Dollar. This digital Bahamian dollar aims to improve financial inclusion across the archipelago, where traditional banking services are limited. With the Sand Dollar, the Central Bank of the Bahamas seeks to facilitate secure, faster, and cheaper transactions, boosting economic activity in remote areas. This initiative provides a practical case study of how CBDCs can address unique regional challenges and promote economic development.

Other key players include the United States Federal Reserve and the Bank of Japan. The Federal Reserve has taken a measured approach, focusing on research and collaboration with academic and financial institutions. They have not yet committed to issuing a digital dollar but emphasize the importance of preparedness to maintain the dollar's global dominance. The Bank of Japan similarly engages in rigorous research and experimentation, reflecting a cautious but proactive stance on CBDCs.

The leadership in CBDC initiatives showcases varied motivations—ranging from enhancing financial inclusion to reinforcing economic sovereignty and control. Meanwhile, these initiatives also carry profound implications for individual privacy and freedom. The centralized nature of CBDCs inherently expands governmental oversight and potentially paves the way for more intrusive monitoring of financial activities.

As leading countries forge ahead with digital currency projects, the tension between technological advancement and civil liberties becomes ever more pronounced. The future landscape of CBDCs will likely influence global financial systems and individual freedoms in ways that are yet to be fully understood. How these dynamics unfold will be critical in shaping the broader 2030 Agenda and its impact on society.

Key Players Globally

When it comes to Central Bank Digital Currencies (CBDCs), several countries are leading the charge, each with unique strategies and ambitions. These key players span various continents, reflecting the global interest and urgency surrounding the digital transformation of financial systems. This section delves into the prominent nations pioneering CBDC initiatives, examining their motivations, progress, and potential implications for the global financial landscape.

China stands at the forefront with its digital yuan, also known as the Digital Currency Electronic Payment (DCEP). Since its pilot program launch in 2020, China has aggressively pushed for the widespread adoption of its digital currency. The People's Bank of China (PBoC) has conducted numerous trials in major cities, involving millions of users and numerous financial transactions. China's intent behind this robust push appears twofold: to gain a competitive edge in the global market and to enhance governmental control over the financial ecosystem.

The European Union, particularly through the efforts of the European Central Bank (ECB), is also deeply invested in the CBDC race. The ECB has laid considerable groundwork for the digital euro, with the primary goal of preserving monetary sovereignty in an increasingly digital world. Given Europe's diverse financial systems and regulatory environments, the challenge lies in cohesively integrating a digital currency across multiple nations. However, the ECB seems committed to making this a reality, acknowledging that failure to do so could leave Europe dependent on foreign or private digital currencies, potentially compromising its financial autonomy.

In North America, the United States has been relatively cautious but is gradually warming up to the idea of a digital dollar. The Federal Reserve has published discussion papers outlining the potential benefits and risks of a CBDC. While no formal decision has been made, there is clear momentum towards exploring its feasibility. The U.S. aims to ensure any such system upholds privacy and combats financial crime, highlighting a deliberate and measured approach to what could be a landmark shift in its monetary policy.

Japan, too, has entered the fray with its own explorations into digital currency. The Bank of Japan (BoJ) has been conducting proof-of-concept experiments for a viable CBDC framework. Japan's efforts are often seen as a response to both internal demands for more efficient payment systems and external pressures from the advancements of neighboring China. The BoJ's cautious yet thorough investigations reflect Japan's intent to evolve its financial systems without compromising stability.

Crossing into the Caribbean, the Bahamas stands out with its Sand Dollar, which holds the distinction of being one of the first fully operational CBDCs. Launched by the Central Bank of the Bahamas, the Sand Dollar aims to enhance financial inclusion and provide seamless access to digital financial services across the archipelago's islands. This initiative underscores how smaller nations can lead by example in the digital currency arena, leveraging technology to address specific regional challenges.

The list wouldn't be complete without mentioning Sweden and its Riksbank, one of the pioneers in the digital currency space with the e-Krona project. Given the already high penetration of digital payments in Sweden, the transition to a CBDC seems like a natural progression. The Riksbank's endeavors focus on ensuring the continuity and resilience of Sweden's payment systems in a future where physical cash might become obsolete.

Another significant player is India, a country characterized by vast economic diversity and rapid digital adoption. The Reserve Bank of India (RBI) has shown considerable interest in CBDCs as part of its broader digital finance strategy. With a burgeoning fintech sector and a significant unbanked population, a digital rupee could potentially bridge profound financial gaps, driving inclusion while reducing the nation's hefty cash management costs.

Africa is not left out, as Nigeria has made headlines with its eNaira. Launched by the Central Bank of Nigeria, the eNaira aims to complement the existing payment systems and foster broader financial inclusion. The rollout faced some initial hitches, yet it serves as a crucial learning point for other developing nations on how digital currencies can be adapted to local contexts and needs.

Finally, Canada is at a crossroads with its CBDC plans. The Bank of Canada has undertaken extensive research and contemplation regarding a digital Canadian dollar, often emphasizing the need for comprehensive public consultations and rigorous legal frameworks before any launch. Canada's approach aligns with its broader tradition of caution and thoroughness in financial policy making.

In conclusion, the global landscape of CBDC initiatives is richly varied, with each leading country bringing its own set of motivations, technological advancements, and regulatory considerations to the table. As these nations continue to develop and refine their digital currencies, the ripple effects on global finance, privacy, and governmental control will be significant. It is essential to monitor these developments closely, understanding that the emergence of CBDCs represents not just a technological shift, but a profound transformation in how societies perceive and handle money.

Implications of Leadership in CBDCs

Leadership in the realm of Central Bank Digital Currencies (CBDCs) carries profound implications for the future financial landscape and beyond. As leading countries push forward their CBDC initiatives, the repercussions are far-reaching, reshaping not only their domestic economies but also the global financial ecosystem. Territorial strides in CBDCs can modify how money is used, influence global power dynamics, and redefine personal and national financial sovereignty.

One key implication of CBDC leadership is the potential for enhanced financial inclusion. Proponents argue that CBDCs can provide unbanked and underbanked populations with direct access to digital financial services. This could be particularly transformative in developing nations where mobile penetration is high but access to traditional banking is limited. The deployment of CBDCs in these contexts may bridge gaps, leading to more equitable economic opportunities.

However, the flipside of this inclusion is an unprecedented level of state surveillance and control. CBDCs, by their digital nature, are inherently trackable. This means that every transaction can be monitored, recorded, and even controlled by central authorities. The leadership of nation-states in CBDC initiatives, therefore, introduces a dual-edged sword: while financial inclusion may improve, individual financial privacy may erode. Governments could potentially use this technology to implement restrictive financial controls, impose fines instantly, or even freeze assets without due process.

Another important implication is the realignment of global financial power. Current global financial powerhouses—like the US with its dollar's dominance—face challenges from emerging CBDCs. If countries such as China successfully implement their digital yuan and achieve widespread adoption, it could undermine the US dollar's position as the world's reserve currency. This shift could diminish the US's influence on the global stage, transferring power to the early adopters of successful CBDC systems.

Beyond power dynamics, leadership in CBDC initiatives could redefine monetary policy effectiveness. Traditional monetary policy tools such as interest rates and reserve requirements may evolve or be replaced by more granular and direct mechanisms. Central banks could potentially implement negative interest rates more effectively by controlling digital wallets directly, influencing people to spend rather than save in economically challenging times.

Moreover, the immediate settlement of transactions facilitated by CBDCs can increase the efficiency and security of payment systems. Cross-border transactions, which currently involve a maze of intermediaries and prolonged settlement periods, could become instantaneous and less costly. However, this increased efficiency also poses risks if different CBDC systems are not interoperable or if geopolitical tensions lead to bifurcated financial systems, complicating global trade and finance.

As leading countries forge ahead with CBDC implementation, the competitive landscape for technology and infrastructure providers will also shift. Countries in the vanguard will likely foster environments ripe for innovation, creating new entrepreneurial and tech development opportunities. However, this shift could also lead to increased digital divides, where countries lagging in CBDC technology and infrastructure find themselves at a disadvantage, both economically and technologically.

The rise of CBDCs raises significant regulatory and legal questions. Will traditional banking regulations suffice, or is there a need for a new regulatory framework to address the unique attributes of digital currencies? Countries leading in CBDC initiatives will set precedents in regulatory matters that could have long-lasting global effects. They will likely influence international standards and practices concerning anti-money laundering (AML) and combating the financing of terrorism (CFT).

From a societal perspective, the new financial ecosystem enabled by CBDCs could reshape the way individuals interact with money. Cash, a bearer instrument that provides anonymity, could become obsolete. In its place, digital currencies could foster a cashless society where every transaction is visible to central authorities. This transition could be disconcerting for those who value financial privacy and autonomy.

Lastly, on the geopolitical front, the leadership in CBDCs might act as a soft power tool. Countries with successful CBDC models could exert influence over their neighbors and even beyond, with their systems becoming models to emulate. The domestic success of a CBDC could become a significant factor in a nation's geopolitical strategy, extending their influence through technological and economic means.

In conclusion, the implications of leadership in CBDCs stretch beyond mere financial innovation. They touch on issues of privacy, power dynamics, regulatory frameworks, societal change, and geopolitical influence. As various countries march forward with their CBDC initiatives, it's essential to scrutinize these developments critically. The stakes are high, and the outcomes, both positive and negative, could shape the global economic landscape for decades to come.

Chapter 10:
Scoring and Ranking: The Social Credit System

The idea of a social credit system is not new, but its implementation in the modern digital age is as captivating as it is alarming. Essentially, a social credit system aims to track and evaluate the behavior of individuals and entities. This system assigns scores based on compliance with societal norms and governmental expectations. These scores can, in turn, influence access to services, employment, and even social standing.

Imagine a world where every action you take, from paying your bills on time to the books you borrow from the library, is monitored and judged. Digital footprints become the essence of your identity, shaping your opportunities and limitations. The core of this system is mass surveillance and data collection, ostensibly to create a more harmonious society. However, the ramifications are far-reaching and often sinister.

Under a social credit system, individual freedom takes a backseat to collective conformity. You are incentivized to behave in ways that the government deems acceptable, lest you face severe consequences. Low scores might mean restricted travel, limited borrowing power, and even social ostracism. Imagine being unable to book a hotel room or buy a train ticket simply because you were critical of governmental policies online.

Critics argue that such systems turn citizens into mere data points and undermine democratic principles. They emphasize the potential for abuse, where governments can manipulate scores for political purposes or target dissidents. The lack of transparency and oversight further erodes public trust, making people feel like they are perpetually under a digital microscope. A system intended to reward trustworthiness instead breeds an environment of fear and obedience.

The global implications of adopting social credit systems are substantial. If one nation sets a precedent, others might follow, creating a domino effect. Corporations could find themselves compelled to align with these systems to maintain good relationships with governments. This would mean an increased level of corporate surveillance over employees and consumers alike. The digital age makes geographical borders almost irrelevant when it comes to data collection and usage, amplifying the reach of such systems across continents.

There's also the aspect of digital inclusion versus exclusion. Those who are less tech-savvy or unwilling to participate in the digital panopticon might find themselves disadvantaged. Digital divides could widen, exacerbating existing inequalities. A social credit system might claim to offer fairer treatment, but it often ends up perpetuating the very biases it aims to eliminate.

The potential of social credit systems to influence global governance cannot be understated. Imagine a world where international travel, trade, and even diplomatic relations are influenced by social credit scores. Nations could use these systems as tools for exerting soft power or applying pressure in international politics. The shift from traditional power structures to those controlled by data and algorithms changes the very fabric of international relations.

While proponents argue that social credit systems enhance civic responsibility and societal harmony, the dark possibilities must be acknowledged. The journey toward such a system is one paved with ethical dilemmas and human rights concerns. What might begin as a mechanism for better societal functioning might soon reveal itself as an instrument of control and repression.

As we delve deeper into the nuances of these systems, it becomes imperative to question the balance between societal good and individual freedom. The specter of a highly controlled society, defined by scores and rankings, should prompt urgent discourse about the road we're heading down. The time to voice these concerns and act upon them is now, before we find ourselves irrevocably submerged in a dystopian reality.

Concept of Social Credit Systems

The Social Credit System is one of the most eerie instruments of control in the modern age, a harrowing mechanism of governance that seeks to extend its reach directly into the lives of individuals. It emerges from the logical progression of digital technologies intertwining with the age-old desire by governments to monitor and influence citizen behavior. The concept itself is deceptively simple: a system that scores individuals based on their actions, behaviors, and even thoughts, rewarding those who conform to state-approved norms while penalizing those who don't.

At its core, the Social Credit System is a centralized, digital ledger of one's social behaviors. Imagine a comprehensive file, continually updated, reflecting every facet of your activities. Not just financial transactions or criminal records, but what books you read, what you post on social media, your shopping habits, and even the company you keep. Through a sophisticated algorithm, each behavior is assigned a value, cumulatively forming your social credit score, a numerical indicator of your trustworthiness and societal value.

This system aspires to be omniscient, leveraging big data, machine learning, and artificial intelligence to aggregate and analyze any piece of information that can be gleaned from your digital footprint. The goal is to incentivize ideal citizenship. High scores may grant someone access to better loans, housing, and even the privilege to travel. Conversely, low scores can lead to public shaming, restricted travel, and exclusion from certain societal benefits—essentially turning individuals into pariahs within their own communities.

The global implications of such a system are significant and far-reaching. First and foremost, it fundamentally shifts the relationship between the state and the individual. Traditional notions of privacy become obsolete, as every action, no matter how minor, is scrutinized and recorded. The concept of sanctuary, a place where one can act freely without fear of repercussion, would be obliterated. In an ironic twist, the very technologies that promised us greater freedom and interconnectedness are being inverted into tools of surveillance and control.

In a Social Credit System, trust is no longer earned through personal interactions and societal contributions alone. Instead, trustworthiness becomes a commodity quantified and regulated by the state. The ramifications extend beyond the individual, affecting businesses, communities, and even international relations. Corporations may manipulate their operations to align with state directives, wary of receiving poor social credit scores that might limit their access to markets or resources.

This system contributes to a climate of perpetual self-censorship. Knowing that every action is monitored could lead individuals to consistently second-guess their choices, curbing expressions of dissent and fostering a homogenized, compliant society. Under such conditions, individuality and critical thought, the very foundations of democratic culture, could be eroded.

One must also consider the technological infrastructure required to support such a system. Advanced AI and machine learning algorithms need to process unimaginable amounts of data in real time. The data must be not just collected, but also interpreted and weighted correctly to ensure that scores reflect a comprehensive yet nuanced view of an individual's societal value. Such sophistication requires massive financial investment and technical expertise, creating a chilling prospect that only the most powerful and resource-rich states can effectively implement such a system.

Yet, beyond the technological challenges lies a more insidious issue: the manipulation of social credit systems for political ends. When the power to score and rank citizens becomes centralized, it can be harnessed to subdue opposition and enforce conformity. Dissent isn't just met with traditional consequences like imprisonment or exile. Instead, it results in systemic and societal ostracization, effectively silencing detractors without public outcry or obvious brutality. The chilling effect on political activism and social movements cannot be overstated.

Additionally, the concept of Social Credit Systems brings ethical concerns that need addressing. The transparency of the scoring process is often questionable. Who controls the algorithm? What constitutes good or bad behavior? These questions highlight the complex moral terrain navigated by such systems. Decisions made by opaque algorithms risk perpetuating biases and injustices, especially if the metrics used to score behaviors are themselves products of flawed or discriminatory notions.

In an interconnected world, the adoption of Social Credit Systems by one state can pressure others to follow suit. The international competition for technological supremacy may compel nations to leverage similar systems in the name of efficiency or security, perpetuating a cycle where individual freedoms are increasingly compromised for the perceived greater good.

The Social Credit System's influence extends far beyond surveillance; it's a mechanism designed to mold society according to a predefined ideal. By rewarding acceptable behaviors and punishing deviance, the system endeavors to craft a populace that operates within tightly controlled boundaries. It involves not just the observation of actions but the manipulation of motivations and desires, subtly enforcing compliance through a combination of promise and peril.

Ultimately, while the Social Credit System may be presented under the guise of societal betterment and improved governance, it serves as a cautionary tale. It shows how technology can be wielded to undermine personal freedoms and reshape societal structures in ways that are both profound and unsettling. As we edge closer to the ambitious goals set out by the 2030 Agenda, understanding and scrutinizing systems of social control has never been more crucial. We must vigilantly safeguard against the encroachment of such mechanisms, lest we find ourselves irrevocably altered by their pervasive influence.

Global Implications

As we delve into the global implications of social credit systems, it's essential to understand that while the concept may be relatively new, its potential impact spans across borders and societal norms. In essence, social credit systems operate by scoring and ranking individuals based on their behaviors, financial activities, and social interactions. These scores can determine access to services, career opportunities, and even personal freedoms.

The adoption of such systems on a worldwide scale would mean a profound shift in how societies operate. Imagine a world where your credit score is not only about your financial credibility but also about your social desirability and governmental compliance. This shift could erode the foundation of personal freedom and autonomy. Countries with varied political systems, from democracies to autocracies, are investigating how social credit systems could serve their interests, thereby raising significant ethical and practical questions.

One stark implication is the potential for increased government control. By leveraging social credit systems, governments can closely monitor and regulate the public's behavior, essentially exerting a vice-like grip on personal freedoms. Citizens might find themselves compelled to conform to state dictates to retain access to basic services. This kind of pervasive oversight is not merely a hypothetical scenario; it's a looming reality given the trajectories in technological advancements and state capabilities.

The global implications also extend to international relations and geopolitics. Nations with restrictive social credit systems could project their ideologies onto weaker states via economic or technological partnerships. This could lead to a domino effect where more countries adopt these systems, not out of intrinsic desire but as a means of keeping pace with global peers. These imposed systems would further cement state power over individual liberties, creating a global framework that prioritizes collective compliance over individual rights.

Moreover, multinational corporations could be influenced by these systems, altering their ways of functioning to align with government standards, thereby affecting global markets. Companies desperate to maintain favorable social credit scores might prioritize state-approved behavior, potentially leading to ethical compromises. Global trade could shift; businesses may choose partners based on their adherence to these standards, rather than merit or quality.

In regions where social credit systems are fully integrated, citizens might face unprecedented scrutiny. For instance, behaviors previously considered private matters, such as buying habits or social associations, could be scrutinized and scored. This would not only alter social dynamics but might also lead to self-censorship and a homogenization of behavior. The diverse tapestry of human interactions could be reduced to algorithmically approved actions.

The global implications also bear significant legal dimensions. International human rights frameworks may struggle to adapt to the new challenges posed by social credit systems. The right to privacy, freedom of expression, and even freedom of movement could be curtailed under the guise of maintaining societal order and security. Legal battles could proliferate as individuals and advocacy groups fight against perceived overreach and demand accountability.

The potential for misuse and discrimination is another grave concern. Marginalized communities could be disproportionately affected, facing systemic disadvantages perpetuated by biased algorithms. Suppose a government were to exploit social credit systems to suppress dissent; in that case, the global community might witness an increase in politically motivated actions against activists, journalists, and opposition figures.

On the economic front, global investment strategies might shift. Investors could factor social credit systems into their risk assessments, potentially isolating countries that deploy draconian measures. Conversely, nations with harmonious social credit scores might attract more foreign direct investments, creating an environment where economic powerhouses have the leverage to shape international norms and standards.

Education systems worldwide could also be influenced. With an emphasis on producing "socially creditworthy" citizens, curricula might adapt to teach behaviors and ideologies that align with favorable scoring metrics. This could limit intellectual diversity and critical thinking, nurturing generations of individuals conditioned to conform rather than innovate.

Ironically, while aiming for societal stability, these systems might breed an undercurrent of distrust. People might second-guess their interactions, fearing the repercussions of a low social credit score. Communities—traditionally bound by organic social bonds—could fracture under the weight of algorithmic judgments, leading to a more isolated and atomized populace.

Finally, resistance to these systems could foster solidarity amongst global communities. Civil societies might find common ground, advocating for the preservation of personal freedoms against encroaching state control. International coalitions and advocacy groups could emerge, challenging the integration and expansion of social credit systems, striving to maintain a balance between technological advancement and individual liberties.

In conclusion, the global implications of social credit systems extend far beyond their intended scope. From governmental control and individual freedoms to economic strategies and social dynamics, these systems have the potential to fundamentally transform the world as we know it. While they may promise order and efficiency, the underlying risks and ethical dilemmas make them a double-edged sword. As we march toward a future shaped by technology and big data, it is imperative to critically examine these systems and advocate for a world where individual freedoms and personal privacy remain paramount.

Chapter 11:
China's Social Credit System:
A Case Study

China's social credit system serves as a formidable example of how governance and technology can intertwine to exert unprecedented control over a population. Introduced with the stated intent to enhance trust within society, this system meticulously tracks, assesses, and publicly rates the behavior of over a billion Chinese citizens and companies.

The functioning of China's system is both complex and far-reaching. Far from being a mere financial credit score, the social credit system incorporates a wide array of factors ranging from financial transactions to personal behaviors. Imagine a world where your everyday activities—like paying bills on time, adhering to traffic laws, and even the type of groceries you purchase—are all used to determine your social credit score. High scores can grant you faster access to loans, better job prospects, and easier travel, while low scores can result in restricted travel, diminished employment opportunities, and public shaming.

The technology driving this system is sophisticated, relying heavily on a vast network of surveillance cameras equipped with facial recognition capabilities, big data analytics, and AI algorithms. These components collectively capture and analyze massive amounts of data in real-time, continually updating each citizen's score. China's social credit machinery echoes Orwellian overtones, establishing a milieu where people are under constant scrutiny.

Real-world examples illustrate just how invasive and impactful China's social credit system can be. Take, for instance, the case of dog ownership. In certain Chinese cities, owning a dog entails more than ensuring it's licensed and vaccinated; the owner's social credit score must also meet or exceed a specific threshold. With stricter regulations, a lower credit score might lead to the confiscation of a beloved pet, emphasizing compliance and societal control over individual rights.

Travel restrictions form another stark element of China's social credit apparatus. Individuals with low scores can find themselves blocked from purchasing plane or train tickets. This restriction effectively confines them within certain geographical boundaries, closely linking personal liberties with behavior as deemed acceptable by the state. Reports have estimated that millions of citizens have been barred from flying or traveling via high-speed rail due to low social credit scores, shedding light on the punitive nature of this system.

Critics argue that the social credit system creates a culture imbued with fear and self-censorship. People are compelled to conform to the prescribed behaviors out of necessity, stripping away the nuances of free will and stifling dissent. Fear of losing points, and consequently freedoms, guides citizens to act in ways that may not align with their personal beliefs but ensure their score remains high.

The concept of social credit is not inherently malevolent. A society where trust and accountability thrive sounds ideal; however, China's implementation verges on dystopian, revealing a mechanism more concerned with control than credit. As one delves deeper into the workings of China's social credit system, it becomes increasingly clear how this concept aligns with the larger narrative of the 2030 Agenda. The broader implications for other nations considering similar systems pose unsettling questions about the trajectory towards global governance and individual freedoms.

Functioning of China's System

The functioning of China's social credit system is a complex yet highly orchestrated framework designed to monitor, evaluate, and influence the behavior of its citizens. At its core, this system amalgamates data from various sources, including financial transactions, social media activities, and even behavioral patterns observed through public surveillance, into a single, quantifiable score. This score serves as a gauge of an individual's trustworthiness and social reliability.

The infrastructure underpinning this system comprises a vast network of interconnected databases managed by both government agencies and private companies. These entities collaborate to amass an exhaustive array of data points, which are processed and analyzed using sophisticated algorithms. In essence, it's a collusion between state and corporate sectors aimed at ensuring compliance and loyalty to state objectives.

Scores in this system can fluctuate based on a range of actions, from paying bills on time to what one posts on social media. For instance, positive actions such as volunteering or making charity donations can enhance one's score, whereas negative behaviors like jaywalking or dissenting posts can lead to deductions. The variability of these scores impacts an individual's social mobility, where a high score can unlock better job prospects, travel allowances, and even dating opportunities, while a low score might result in penalties such as travel bans or reduced access to public services.

Public surveillance plays a critical role in the ongoing assessment of each citizen's score. Across Chinese cities, thousands of surveillance cameras equipped with facial recognition technology operate round-the-clock. These cameras feed real-time data into centralized systems, where individuals can be singled out for both positive and negative actions. The government also encourages a culture of mutual surveillance, where citizens report each other's behaviors, effectively making everyone both a watchdog and a subject.

The bureaucracy involved in managing the social credit system is immense. Various government bodies hold responsibilities for different aspects. The National Development and Reform Commission (NDRC) oversees the broad framework, while local governments implement and adjust rules based on regional specifics. This multi-tiered approach ensures that the system remains flexible enough to accommodate diverse sociopolitical environments while adhering to overall state objectives.

One of the system's most insidious components is the "blacklist" mechanism. Individuals with persistently low scores are added to these blacklists, which are shared across agencies and private entities. This makes life increasingly difficult for the blacklisted, as they face a series of restrictions ranging from reduced employment opportunities to limitations on renting property. This effectively turns social ostracism into a state-sanctioned punishment mechanism.

Critics argue that the social credit system is a modern-day Orwellian construct designed to stifle dissent and manufacture a homogenized society. They emphasize that it extends the government's reach into the private lives of citizens in unprecedented ways, curtailing freedoms and enforcing a rigid, state-approved moral code. The lack of transparency and recourse further exacerbates these issues, leaving individuals with little to no means to contest their scores or understand the criteria behind them.

Beyond the individual level, the system also exercises control over corporate entities. Companies, both domestic and foreign, are subject to their own credit ratings. These ratings are influenced by compliance with government regulations, labor practices, and even business dealings. High-scoring companies receive benefits like easier access to loans and favorable terms in government tenders, while lower-scoring firms might face audits, fines, or operational restrictions. This extends the state's influence into the economic realm, ensuring that businesses adhere to national priorities and policies.

Technological advancements are continually being integrated to make the system more efficient and pervasive. Artificial intelligence and big data analytics are used to identify patterns and predict behaviors, making it possible to pre-emptively reward or sanction citizens. These technologies make the system not just a reactive mechanism but a proactive tool in shaping societal behavior.

Despite its many facets, the core objective of China's social credit system remains clear: to create a socially cohesive and compliant society. By meticulously tracking and influencing individual and collective actions, the state ensures that its vision of order and control is met. However, this comes at the cost of individual freedom and privacy, raising questions about the moral and ethical implications of such an extensive surveillance apparatus.

In shaping this system, China sets a daunting precedent for other nations contemplating similar forms of social monitoring. As aspects of the social credit system find resonance in other regulatory environments around the world, the global implications become increasingly concerning. This system is a stark reflection of the growing intertwinement of governance, technology, and societal control, showcasing what the future could hold if such models are pursued uncritically.

Understanding the functioning of China's social credit system offers insights into the potential extremes of state control, painting a vivid picture of how technology and governance can arguably, when combined, infringe upon personal freedoms. In this context, China's system acts as a case study that warns of the possible trajectories other nations might follow if similar frameworks are adopted.

Real-world Examples: Dog Confiscation and Travel Restrictions

China's Social Credit System has created a myriad of real-world implications, some of which appear almost dystopian in their severity. One of the most striking examples is the state's approach to dog ownership. In some regions, particularly those urban locales with high social credit enforcement, citizens are subject to strict regulations concerning their pets. A resident's social credit score can influence their eligibility to own certain breeds of dogs, with specific guidelines dictating ownership rights. If an individual's score falls below an acceptable threshold, their pets can be confiscated by authorities.

Consider a city like Jinan, where rules around pet ownership are enforced rigorously. Residents must adhere to a strict code: dogs must be registered, vaccinated, and microchipped. Failure to comply can result in fines and the deduction of social credit points. In more severe cases, animals are taken from their homes. These actions are justified by the government as necessary for public safety and welfare but are widely seen as punitive measures designed to control and coerce behavior conforming to state expectations.

The process is not usually immediate; it begins with warnings and fines. For example, if an individual is caught walking their dog without a leash, this would trigger a warning and a reduction in their social credit score. Repeat offenses lead to higher penalties, and persistent non-compliance could result in the dog being seized. Pet owners, therefore, must ensure they are always compliant lest they risk losing their beloved pets. The fear of losing a pet, which for many is considered a family member, coerces individuals into a state of constant vigilance and adherence to the rules imposed by the social credit system.

Beyond pet ownership, travel restrictions are another arena where the severity of China's social credit system becomes evident. Citizens with low social credit scores can find themselves barred from purchasing airline tickets or accessing high-speed train services. This aspect of the system is particularly effective in a country where speedy travel options are critical due to the vast distances between major cities.

Travel bans are implemented for various reasons. Defaulting on a loan, failing to pay fines, or engaging in behaviors deemed inappropriate—such as public drunkenness or spreading false information online—can trigger these restrictions. Once flagged by the system, individuals may find themselves unable to leave their hometowns. This geographic stifling impacts not only personal freedom but also economic opportunities, as people are unable to attend job interviews, business meetings, or even family gatherings in other regions.

Consider the case of Liu Hu, a Chinese journalist who was blacklisted for his criticism of the government. With a low social credit score, Liu was restricted from buying plane tickets, thus hampering his ability to work and travel. Such restrictions serve as powerful tools to silence dissent and maintain a compliant populace. The case of Liu Hu illustrates how the social credit system reaches beyond mere financial repercussions to more deeply affect personal autonomy and freedom of expression.

Instances of travel restrictions are often exacerbated by the comprehensive surveillance network underpinning the social credit system. Facial recognition technology, coupled with extensive data collection from various sources, ensures that individuals cannot easily circumvent the rules. This network allows the government to quickly and efficiently monitor and enforce travel bans, making it nearly impossible for flagged individuals to evade their penalties.

The repercussions of these restrictions extend into social isolation. People who can't travel may find it difficult to maintain relationships with family and friends living far away. This isolation can create a psychological burden, increasing stress and decreasing overall well-being. In a society where maintaining social connections is vital, such restrictions can be deeply damaging.

Moreover, the interplay between dog confiscation and travel restrictions paints a broader picture of control that permeates through various aspects of daily life. Both examples underscore a fundamental strategy: to manipulate and adjust citizen behavior by tying actions to a system of rewards and penalties. This underpins much of the rationale behind the social credit system: the creation of a populace that self-regulates in line with government-defined moral and social standards.

In conclusion, the examples of dog confiscation and travel restrictions within China's social credit system highlight the lengths to which a government can go to enforce conformity and compliance. These real-world impacts offer a glimpse into a future where personal freedoms are significantly curtailed under the guise of public safety and order. Understanding these examples brings us one step closer to grasping the broader implications of the 2030 agenda, urging us all to critically assess and resist any encroachment on personal liberties.

Chapter 12:
Impacts on Daily Life and
Personal Freedom

The sweeping changes proposed under the 2030 Agenda present both an intriguing and unsettling transformation of daily life. At its core, the agenda promises to reshape how individuals interact with governments, corporations, and even each other. While touted as a stride towards sustainability and equality, certain aspects of these goals may inadvertently impinge on personal freedoms.

The integration of digital ID systems, for instance, brings a layer of convenience in accessing services. However, it also opens up significant privacy concerns. Imagine a world where every move is tracked, every transaction is recorded, and every interaction is evaluated. The prospect of having your entire life cataloged by an unseen digital eye is far from comforting.

Perhaps the most poignant impact of the 2030 Agenda is the erosion of individual autonomy. Imagine having your choices scrutinized and ranked by an opaque social credit system. Your access to amenities, loans, and even travel could be influenced by this score. This kind of control veers dangerously close to an Orwellian nightmare, where each decision must align with a state-sanctioned directive.

While economic adjustments are necessary for envisioning a sustainable future, forced changes in personal ownership suggest moving towards rental models for assets such as homes and vehicles. This shift towards a 'shared economy,' under the guise of efficiency and conservation, sounds paradoxical to the long-held notion of personal ownership—a symbolic and practical manifestation of freedom.

On a more granular level, the daily experience of life will undoubtedly change. You might find grocery shopping altered by restrictions on what can and cannot be bought. Labeling regulations, quotas on certain types of foods, and the limitation on 'non-essential' items could become the norm. What we once took for granted as personal choices—like our diet—could be regimented by distant policymakers.

Working life will also experience shifts that raise questions about personal freedom. The move towards gig economies and less stable work environments is framed as adaptive and progressive. While flexibility in employment can be seen as a positive, the lack of job security counters this benefit, compelling individuals to accept any available work, regardless of quality or safety.

Community life and social interactions could undergo a significant metamorphosis. With centralized systems deciding what constitutes 'acceptable' social behavior, grassroots culture and local traditions risk being homogenized. The potential of losing cultural diversity in favor of a monolithic societal structure is a genuine concern.

Your freedom of speech and expression will not be exempt from scrutiny. The increasing control over social media and public discourse could lead to a sanitized and polarized environment. Dissenting voices might find themselves silenced or marginalized, marking a chilling drift away from democratic values.

In essence, while the 2030 Agenda aims for a reinvigorated world order, it simultaneously risks curtailing the essence of individual freedom. The roadmap to sustainability and equality is paved with policies that, if unchecked, could lead to a future where personal choices are limited, and freedom is but an illusion.

Understanding these impacts is crucial for weighing the benefits against the potential costs. Awareness and critical thought are vital in navigating this complex landscape, ensuring that the sacrifices we make today do not lead to a constrained tomorrow.

Examples of Restricted Freedoms

Life as we know it pivots around our ability to make choices, from the mundane to the significant. However, under the 2030 Agenda, many of these freedoms are likely to be curtailed. One glaring example is freedom of movement. Traditionally, hopping in your car or booking a flight has been a straightforward process. But with expected regulations related to carbon footprints, travel might involve a complex web of permissions and credits, tightly controlled by governing bodies.

When it comes to property ownership, the picture is even more grim. The concept of "You will own nothing and be happy" isn't just a catchphrase—it's a harbinger of enforced communal ownership structures. Homes, cars, and even personal items could transition from private ownership to shared resources, significantly altering how people perceive and experience personal space. Imagine living in a house that isn't yours, driving a car that's just temporarily at your disposal, and having almost all personal assets subjected to communal use.

Food and water, basic necessities for survival, aren't spared either. Nations could enforce stringent regulations on water usage and impose quotas on food consumption. Agricultural practices would be transformed, with individual farmers potentially losing their autonomy in deciding what crops to grow and when. Instead, they might operate under directives aimed at meeting global sustainability goals, thereby restricting local innovation and self-sufficiency.

Education systems demonstrate another facet of restriction. Curricula would be overhauled to align with the global objectives set out by the agenda. Local traditions and teachings may become obsolete, replaced by a homogenized, globalized education model. While there's an argument to be made for uniform standards, this centralized control could eliminate the cultural richness and diversity that define communities.

Digital surveillance also rears its ugly head. In a world where personal identification and financial transactions are tightly monitored through Digital IDs and Central Bank Digital Currencies (CBDCs), your every move is traceable. This surveillance infrastructure promises safety but at the cost of your privacy. Anonymity might become a relic of the past, with every purchase, journey, or online activity logged and stored in a government's data bank.

The concept of a social credit system, already functional in some parts of the world, could expand globally. Imagine a future where your behavior, social interactions, and even health choices directly impact your social standing and access to services. A poor credit score might mean restricted access to travel, employment opportunities, or even educational institutions. The implications for personal freedom are vast and terrifying.

Freedom of speech, a cornerstone of democratic societies, wouldn't escape unscathed. Platforms for public discourse could face severe limitations. Content that doesn't align with the approved narratives may be censored or removed, leaving citizens with a controlled flow of information. The age of freewheeling debate could give way to an era where dissent is not tolerated, and compliance is strictly enforced.

Medical freedom, too, is at risk. Under the guise of public health safety, mandatory medical procedures and treatments might become the norm. Personal choices about health and body autonomy could be surrendered to overarching health mandates. The implications are far-reaching, as individuals would have limited say in their own medical decisions.

These restricted freedoms cast a shadow over artistic and creative expressions as well. Art, literature, and other forms of creativity that do not conform to the global agenda's principles could be stifled. It's not far-fetched to imagine a future where creative works are subjected to approval processes, putting a damper on the freedom artists currently enjoy.

Religious practices, too, might not be insulated from these sweeping changes. Aligning religious doctrines and practices with global peace and sustainability goals could usher in restrictions on certain religious freedoms. Worship, assembly, and the expression of beliefs might be filtered through the lens of global governance, losing their inherent sanctity and individuality.

The constraints don't end here. Freedoms related to family life could also come under scrutiny. Governments might impose guidelines on family size under the pretext of population control for environmental sustainability. Policies could dictate how many children one can have, the kind of upbringing they should receive, and even the type of education they must be exposed to, heavily influencing family dynamics and personal life choices.

Economic freedom is yet another casualty. With centralized control over currencies and financial systems, economic activities could be subjected to monitoring and manipulation. Personal wealth could become an abstract concept, with savings and investments tightly controlled or outright discouraged in favor of state-controlled financial schemes. This could stifle entrepreneurship and innovation, creating a society where financial liberation is but a memory.

In summary, the 2030 Agenda's vision threatens to impinge upon various facets of personal freedom. From the most intimate choices regarding your body and family, the food you eat, and the information you consume, to the broader considerations of how you express yourself and interact with the world. The cascading effect of these restricted freedoms introduces a new world order that prioritizes collective sustainability over individual autonomy, fundamentally altering the human experience as we know it.

Global Repercussions

The 2030 Agenda's reach doesn't just stop at individual nations; its impact ripples across the globe, altering the way we think, live, and govern ourselves. Consider how digital ID systems, which claim to streamline everything from healthcare to voting, introduce new layers of control over citizens. While proponents laud the efficiency and potential to combat fraud, the sinister side is often understated. What happens when your entire identity is governed by a digital system that could potentially be manipulated or hacked? It's not just an invasion of privacy; it's a breach that resonates worldwide.

Economic repercussions are another significant facet. Central Bank Digital Currencies (CBDCs) are at the frontline of this change. Countries leading the charge in CBDC implementation can wield enormous power over global financial systems. If a government can monitor and restrict how you spend your money, imagine the leverage this offers them on an international scale. Financial autonomy becomes a relic of the past, and nations could find themselves at the mercy of a few central authorities.

And it's not just personal finance that's under threat. International trade can also become a playground for these digital currencies.

Countries resistant to adopting such measures may find themselves excluded from global markets or punished via economic sanctions orchestrated through a unified digital currency system. What used to be sovereign decisions over a nation's own currency can be overridden by larger global networks of power, causing a ripple effect that impacts smaller nations disproportionately.

Social Credit Systems might seem like distant threats, confined to authoritarian regimes like China. However, the subtle introduction of similar scoring mechanisms in democratic nations is cause for concern. These systems can easily be adopted and repurposed, shaping the behavior of individuals on a mass scale. If one's access to essential services or ability to travel is determined by a 'social score,' then freedom as we know it starts to disintegrate. And when one country successfully employs such a system without major resistance, others quickly follow suit.

Moreover, the alignment of major international organizations like the United Nations and the World Economic Forum behind these initiatives amplifies their global impact. The 2030 Agenda is not an isolated mission but a coordinated effort that sees compliance from various countries and businesses. This collaborative push spreads the agenda's influence, often without the explicit consent of the governed. Policies that originate in closed-door meetings among global elites end up trickling down to everyday citizens, thereby altering lives in ways they never anticipated.

Political autonomy becomes another casualty. As nations comply with international goals and standards set by entities like the UN, they relinquish a portion of their sovereignty. Local laws and regulations can be shaped or overridden by international decrees aimed at meeting the 2030 Agenda's objectives. For example, environmental regulations originating from the agenda might force countries into economic policies they wouldn't otherwise adopt, resulting in both benefits and drawbacks. The sovereignty of legislative bodies is undermined by larger, unelected global entities.

Public health directives can also be influenced. In the wake of global health crises, initiatives aligned with the 2030 Agenda can determine the policies countries adopt, often at the cost of personal freedoms. Vaccination mandates, health data sharing, and even quarantine measures can be globally coordinated, stripping nations of their ability to make context-specific decisions. A centralized approach to health care might sound effective theoretically but poses enormous risks of homogenized solutions that may not fit all environments.

The repercussions also surface in areas like education. Curricular changes guided by the 2030 Agenda aim to create a more 'sustainable' citizenry but often end up as vehicles for indoctrination. Nations find themselves compelled to revise educational frameworks to align with global standards. This standardization may stifle local heritage and knowledge systems, pressing students into a one-size-fits-all model. The cultural impact is subtle yet profound, homogenizing disparate educational systems into a global narrative that aligns with specific ideological goals.

In a globalized world where communication transcends borders instantly, media plays a powerful role in shaping public perception. Media conglomerates influenced by the 2030 Agenda can push narratives that homogenize viewpoints, thus controlling the discourse on subjects ranging from climate change to economic policies. Independent and local journalism may struggle to survive under the weight of well-funded global narratives, distorting the public's ability to access a diverse range of opinions.

Legal systems can't escape the reach of global repercussions either. International coalitions and treaties aimed at enforcing the 2030 Agenda's goals might lead to legal reforms that harmonize with global directives but disrupt local legal traditions and practices. Countries sign on to agreements that necessitate the reinterpretation or outright rewriting of their legal codes, forcing compliance through diplomatic and economic pressures.

In conclusion, the global repercussions of the 2030 Agenda are manifold and far-reaching. Economic systems, political autonomy, public health, education, media, and legal frameworks all stand affected. The danger lies not just in the measures themselves but in their ability to interlock and reinforce one another, creating a pervasive system of control that transcends national boundaries. Thus, understanding these global repercussions is crucial as they hold the potential to reshape daily life, personal freedoms, and the world as we know it.

Chapter 13:
Advocating for Personal Choice and Freedom

Freedom is a fundamental human right, yet, in this modern era, it's under siege from various global initiatives. At the heart of these efforts is the 2030 Agenda, which seeks to reshape societal norms and individual liberties under the guise of progress and sustainability. The importance of safeguarding personal choice and freedom has never been more significant. The autonomy to make decisions, govern one's path, and maintain privacy is what makes us inherently human.

Individual liberties are the bedrock of a healthy society. When people can choose how they live, work, and interact, society thrives. But when these freedoms are eroded, even subtly, the impact is profound. Governments and transnational entities often push for centralized control, arguing it's for the greater good. However, history has taught us the dangers of such concentration of power. It leads to suppression, loss of diversity in thought, and ultimately, a dystopian existence.

One strategy to combat the erosion of personal freedoms is through public awareness and education. Information is a powerful tool. Understanding the implications of policies and agendas allows individuals to take an active stance. Grassroots movements and community organizations play a crucial role here. By fostering discussions, they create informed citizens ready to advocate for their rights. These collective voices can challenge overreaches and promote transparency in governance.

Legal frameworks also serve as a cornerstone for preserving freedoms. Constitutional rights need defending, and legal challenges can thwart overbearing regulations. Recent legal battles have shown how vital judiciary systems are in checking the excesses of executive and legislative branches. Vigilance and a willingness to engage the legal process can help protect the integrity of personal choices.

Advocating for personal freedom isn't just about prevention; it's also about preparedness. As technology advances, so too does the potential for surveillance and control. A dual approach of adopting privacy-enhancing technologies while challenging invasive policies is essential. Tools like encryption, decentralized networks, and secure communication platforms can shield individual activities from prying eyes. Concurrently, advocacy for privacy rights needs to be relentless to influence policymakers to craft legislation that protects rather than constrains.

Moreover, individual action is powerful. Simple choices—like supporting businesses that prioritize privacy, participating in local governance, and staying informed about legislative changes—can collectively shape a robust culture of freedom. Personal responsibility in safeguarding one's data and being prudent about the information shared online cannot be overstated. In our interconnected world, every small step towards self-preservation counts.

It's also vital to remain skeptical of narratives that promise utopian outcomes in exchange for little sacrifices. The balance between security and freedom is delicate. A vigilant society questions and critically examines these trade-offs. The promise of collective well-being should not undermine individual autonomy. A forum for healthy debate and discourse is necessary to scrutinize the intentions behind global agendas.

In essence, the struggle for personal choice and freedom is an ongoing battle. The vision for 2030 posits a future where societal compliance may come at the cost of individual liberties. It's incumbent upon each of us to advocate for a future where personal freedom and choice remain sacrosanct, defending them against any tide that seeks to diminish our humanity.

Importance of Individual Liberties

Individual liberties are the bedrock of a free society and essential to the human experience. We thrive best when we have the autonomy to make personal choices and control our own destinies. Yet, under the shadow of the 2030 Agenda, these fundamental freedoms are under siege. When governments and global institutions usurp our decisions on personal matters, they strip away our agency and dignity. The creeping encroachment on individual liberties is not just an affront to personal freedom but a dangerous precedent that undermines the very principles of democracy.

Imagine a world where every action, from the most mundane to the most significant, requires approval from centralized authorities. The 2030 Agenda, with its myriad controls and regulations, advances precisely this dystopian vision. If personal choice is eroded, the essence of self-determination is lost. Individuals would no longer be seen as autonomous agents but as mere cogs in a vast bureaucratic machine. This transformation is not theoretical; it's already happening in some parts of the world.

A stark manifestation of the erosion of individual liberties is the implementation of social credit systems. These systems are designed to monitor, assess, and influence human behavior. Imagine being penalized for violating arbitrary rules or receiving rewards for compliance. Such mechanisms erode personal freedoms by conditioning behavior through surveillance and control. Your liberty becomes contingent on the approval of central authorities, and the intrinsic value of individual choice is reduced to a mere tool for achieving prescribed social behaviors.

The importance of individual liberties extends beyond the abstract realm of ethics into practical, everyday life. Consider the right to privacy, a fundamental aspect of personal freedom. Under massive data collection and digital surveillance programs, individuals lose control over their own personal information. Every click, purchase, and interaction can be tracked, monitored, and potentially used against them. The sanctity of private life disintegrates, leaving individuals exposed and vulnerable.

Freedom of speech is another crucial liberty under threat. In a society dictated by a one-size-fits-all agenda, dissenting voices are often silenced. The suppression of free speech not only stifles individual expression but also impedes societal progress. Diverse viewpoints fuel innovation and adaptation; without them, societies stagnate. The 2030 Agenda's proposed restrictions on free speech in the name of unity or security threaten to create an echo chamber of conformist views, diminishing the richness of public discourse.

Economic freedom, often viewed through the lens of capitalism, is vital to preserving individual liberties. The right to own property, start a business, and engage in free trade empowers individuals to improve their circumstances and contribute to societal prosperity. Economic liberty fosters a sense of responsibility, innovation, and self-worth. When policies advocate for collective ownership or state control, they impair the individual's ability to thrive independently. The notion of "owning nothing and being happy" may sound utopian, but in reality, it leads to dependency and loss of personal agency.

Governments and global organizations often justify intrusions into personal liberties as necessary for the greater good. While the intentions may seem noble, such justifications are fraught with peril.

The balance between collective welfare and individual freedom is delicate, and tipping it too far towards the former can result in authoritarianism. History is replete with examples where the promise of security or prosperity has been used to rationalize the curtailment of personal freedoms, often leading to grievous outcomes.

Individual liberties are also linked to human dignity. The ability to make one's own choices, even if they lead to failure, is an aspect of what it means to live a dignified life. External constraints on this liberty imply that individuals cannot be trusted with their own lives. Such paternalism is both disrespectful and disempowering. It breeds a culture of dependency and submissiveness, contrary to the values of self-reliance and independence that underpin free societies.

The battle for individual liberties must be fought on multiple fronts. Legal frameworks that protect these freedoms are essential. Vigilant citizens who are aware of their rights and ready to defend them are equally important. Activism and advocacy can play pivotal roles in raising awareness and resisting encroachments. By pushing back against policies and mandates that infringe on our liberties, we safeguard not just our own freedoms but those of future generations.

Education plays a critical role in preserving individual liberties as well. Informed citizens are better equipped to recognize and resist attempts to curtail their freedoms. Educational systems must emphasize critical thinking and the importance of personal liberties. Only through understanding and appreciating these freedoms can we hope to maintain them in the face of growing pressures.

Ultimately, the preservation of individual liberties is a shared responsibility. Governments, institutions, and citizens must all play their part. The alternative, a world where personal choice is a relic of the past, is too grim to contemplate. By recognizing the importance of our individual liberties, we take the first step towards a future where freedom and autonomy remain protected, ensuring that we can lead lives of our own choosing.

Strategies for Preservation

Advocating for personal choice and freedom in the face of the 2030 Agenda's sweeping changes requires a multi-faceted approach. Ensuring individual liberties remain intact while global leaders push for comprehensive reforms is no small task. Various strategies can be implemented to preserve personal freedoms and autonomy in this new world order.

First and foremost, education is critical. Informing the public about the implications of the 2030 Agenda and its potential impact on personal freedoms is the foundation of any effective preservation strategy. Awareness campaigns, community meetings, and informative literature play vital roles in this effort. When people understand what's at stake, they can make informed decisions and stand up against policies that threaten their freedoms.

It's essential to engage with local and national governments through advocacy. Writing letters, attending town hall meetings, and organizing peaceful protests can put pressure on elected officials to consider the preservation of individual liberties when enacting new policies. Encouraging grassroots movements can amplify these efforts, as local activism often has a substantial impact on larger political structures.

Legal challenges also serve as a robust strategy for preservation. Legal systems across the world offer various mechanisms to challenge and overturn policies and laws that infringe on personal freedoms. Building alliances with civil liberties organizations and pro-freedom legal groups can provide the necessary support and expertise for these legal battles.

Technology can be both a threat and a tool for preserving freedom. On one hand, digital surveillance and data tracking pose significant risks to privacy. However, the same technologies can be leveraged to safeguard individual freedoms. Decentralized platforms, encryption technologies, and secure communication channels can play crucial roles in protecting personal data and ensuring privacy.

Community self-reliance is another crucial strategy. By building local networks and emphasizing local production, communities can reduce dependency on global supply chains that can be exploited to control populations. Supporting local businesses, growing food locally, and developing community-based financial systems can offer significant resilience against central control.

Collaborating with international coalitions focused on preserving freedoms can amplify efforts. By joining forces with global networks that share common values, communities can gain support, share strategies, and build a more robust defense against policies that threaten individual freedoms.

Personal action also plays a role. Cultivating a mindset of vigilance and resilience within oneself and one's community is critical. This involves staying informed, participating in dialogues, and being proactive rather than reactive. The willingness to adapt and change in response to threats to freedom is vital for long-term preservation.

Media literacy is another essential component. Understanding how media shapes public perception can equip individuals to critically evaluate the information they consume. Encouraging skepticism of media narratives and promoting independent journalism can reduce the influence of biased or misleading information designed to sway public opinion in favor of restrictive policies.

Entrepreneurs and small business owners can contribute to the preservation of personal freedoms by maintaining control over their enterprises and resisting centralization. By fostering innovation and independence in the business sector, they can push back against economic policies designed to consolidate control among a few large entities.

Educational institutions also have a significant role. Curriculum that fosters critical thinking, teaches the importance of freedom, and encourages civic engagement can prepare future generations to value and fight for their liberties. It's essential to counteract indoctrination by providing balanced perspectives and promoting the principles of democracy and individual rights.

Lastly, maintaining an open dialogue about the evolving landscape of personal freedoms is necessary. Regularly discussing potential threats and sharing effective preservation strategies can keep the community engaged and prepared. By staying connected and informed, individuals can collectively navigate the challenges posed by the 2030 Agenda.

Implementing these strategies requires dedication and cooperation at all levels of society. From empowering individuals with knowledge to engaging in legal and political action, every effort matters in the quest to preserve personal choice and freedom. By coming together and utilizing a comprehensive approach, we can safeguard our liberties in the face of sweeping global changes.

Chapter 14:
Economic Freedom and
Personal Ownership

In any free society, economic freedom forms the backbone of personal liberty. It allows individuals to innovate, take risks, and reap the benefits of their hard work. Capitalism, despite its flaws, has been the primary vehicle driving economic growth and innovation for centuries. When people are free to make their own economic decisions, the entire society benefits.

One of the most alarming aspects of the 2030 Agenda is its potential to undermine this economic freedom. Central to this plan are policies that could drastically alter the landscape of personal ownership. Imagine a world where owning property, starting your own business, or even holding a substantial amount of personal wealth is discouraged or controlled by the state. This isn't merely a dystopian scenario; it's part of the vision some proponents of the 2030 Agenda hold.

For many, the idea of "You will own nothing and be happy" seems like a fantastic threat. However, if we look closely at certain policies and proposals, it's clear that there are dangers to our economic freedoms. Central Bank Digital Currencies (CBDCs), for example, offer governments unprecedented control over personal finances. It's not far-fetched to think that such mechanisms could limit your ability to accumulate and use wealth as you see fit.

Economic freedom is not just about the ability to buy and sell goods. It's also about the freedom to choose employment, to innovate, and to have a sense of security that your assets are protected by the rule of law. Threats to economic freedom often manifest as state interventions that seem benign but gradually erode personal autonomy. Under the guise of "greater good," individual rights slowly become privileges that can be revoked.

There is a growing concern that these interventions could lead to a society where personal wealth is increasingly viewed as antithetical to social justice. Redistributive policies, while often intended to reduce inequality, can create environments where incentives to work hard and innovate are diminished. Without the assurance of personal ownership, why would anyone invest time, resources, or effort into entrepreneurial endeavors?

Moreover, the limitation of economic freedom could disproportionately affect small businesses and entrepreneurs. Unlike large corporations with resources to adapt, small businesses often operate on thin margins and are more vulnerable to shifts in policy and economic conditions. The loss of these enterprises would not only impact the economy but also erode local communities and the social fabric they uphold.

While proponents of the 2030 Agenda argue that these measures are necessary for sustainability and social equity, it's crucial to scrutinize the long-term implications. The loss of economic freedom can lead to a concentration of power, undermining the very goals these policies aim to achieve. It becomes a precarious balance, wherein the very tools designed to create equity may, in fact, restrict personal liberties and freedoms.

Preserving economic freedom requires vigilance and active participation from citizens. It's essential to question and challenge policies that threaten personal ownership and autonomy. In doing so, we uphold the principles of a free society where individuals can aspire, innovate, and prosper based on their own merits and ambitions.

As we progress towards the future envisioned by the 2030 Agenda, it is imperative to remain wary of the subtle encroachments on our economic freedom. Understanding these threats and advocating for policies that preserve personal ownership and economic liberty is not just an option but a necessity.

The Role of Capitalism

Capitalism has long been heralded as a driving force for economic freedom and personal ownership. At its core, capitalism thrives on the principles of private property, free markets, and competition. These elements empower individuals to pursue their own economic goals, fostering innovation and wealth creation. Yet, as we delve into the complexities of the 2030 Agenda, it's crucial to examine the potential risks capitalism faces in this evolving landscape.

The traditional capitalistic framework is built upon the idea that individuals have the fundamental right to own and control their property. This extends to businesses, investments, and even intellectual property. This sense of ownership fuels the entrepreneurial spirit that drives much of a nation's economic growth. When individuals are able to own and operate businesses, they not only provide goods and services but also create employment opportunities, contributing to the overall prosperity of society.

Moreover, capitalism relies on the free market system, where supply and demand dictate prices and resource allocation. This creates efficiencies and opportunities for innovation, as companies compete to meet consumer needs better and more cost-effectively than their rivals. In this dynamic environment, the consumer holds significant power, influencing market trends and driving improvements in products and services.

However, the 2030 Agenda, with its broad-reaching goals and centralized initiatives, raises critical questions about the future of capitalism as we know it. One of the most pressing concerns is the potential shift towards greater governmental and organizational control over economic activities. This could manifest in various forms, from increased regulations and taxes to more direct interventions in market operations.

In particular, the notion of "You Will Own Nothing and Be Happy," a phrase often associated with the Great Reset initiative, suggests a paradigm shift away from traditional ownership models. Instead of owning homes, cars, or even certain types of personal property, individuals might increasingly be encouraged—or required—to share resources or access them as a service. While this could offer certain efficiencies and environmental benefits, it also threatens the foundational principle of private ownership that underpins capitalism.

Another facet to consider is the role of large, transnational corporations and their interplay with global governance structures like the World Economic Forum (WEF) and the United Nations (UN). These entities often wield significant influence over national policies and economic strategies. In a capitalist society, competition among businesses usually serves as a check against monopolistic and oligopolistic tendencies. But when corporations align too closely with global governance structures, there's a danger of consolidating power in ways that might stifle competition and diminish the economic freedom of smaller enterprises.

It's important to remember that capitalism, at its best, is a system that empowers individuals. This empowerment extends to consumers who benefit from a variety of choices and to entrepreneurs who can chase their dreams without undue interference. Disrupting this balance by shifting towards a more centralized economic model could lead to a loss of innovation and reduce the overall incentive for productivity. This isn't mere speculation; historical precedents have shown that economies with higher degrees of government control often struggle to achieve the same levels of efficiency and growth as their more capitalist counterparts.

Furthermore, capitalism encourages the accumulation and reinvestment of capital. This reinvestment is vital for technological advancement, infrastructure development, and overall economic expansion. When individuals and businesses have the freedom to invest their resources as they see fit, they contribute to a cycle of growth and prosperity that benefits the wider community. In contrast, centralizing control over these resources could lead to misallocation and inefficiencies that stymie progress.

It's not just about economic metrics, either. The role of capitalism also touches on personal freedoms and self-determination. In a capitalist society, individuals have a greater degree of control over their economic destinies. They can choose their career paths, launch businesses, and invest their money in ways that align with their personal values and goals. Stripping away these choices in favor of a more top-down approach risks alienating individuals from the economic system itself, making them feel like cogs in a machine rather than active participants in an ever-evolving market.

As we navigate the complexities of the 2030 Agenda and its potential impact on capitalism, it's crucial to remain vigilant. The promise of economic equality and environmental sustainability is enticing, but it must be balanced against the need to preserve individual freedoms and economic dynamism. Capitalism, with its inherent capacity for innovation and growth, offers a powerful framework for addressing many of the world's challenges—if we allow it to do so. Resisting the urge to centralize control and maintaining a focus on personal ownership and economic freedom will be vital steps in ensuring that capitalism continues to play its essential role in our society.

In conclusion, capitalism stands as a beacon of economic freedom and personal ownership. Its principles have driven unparalleled growth and innovation, nurturing environments where individuals can prosper and contribute to society. As the 2030 Agenda looms, it's imperative to scrutinize the pathways it proposes carefully. Ensuring that capitalism maintains its foundational elements will be crucial in safeguarding the freedoms and opportunities that lie at the heart of our economic systems. The role of capitalism, therefore, is not just about wealth generation but also about preserving the essence of what it means to be economically free.

Threats to Economic Freedom

As we dive deeper into the 2030 Agenda, it becomes apparent that economic freedom and personal ownership are under siege. The push toward collective ownership and centralized governance threatens the very fabric of what has driven innovation, prosperity, and individual liberty for centuries. The 2030 Agenda implies a paradigm shift that could undermine the principles of capitalism, around which global economic systems have traditionally been built.

Within the context of economic freedom, the concept of personal ownership is intrinsic. Private property rights are not just about possessions but about the freedom to make decisions, plan for the future, and build wealth. However, the specter of global governance poses significant threats to these rights, potentially imposing limitations and redistributing resources in ways that serve broader, potentially less transparent, aims. This could include anything from restrictive property laws to mandatory participation in communal living arrangements.

One of the most immediate threats comes from the idea of wealth redistribution. The 2030 Agenda advocates for equitable distribution of resources, which, in theory, sounds noble. However, in practice, it could mean higher taxes, more stringent regulations on businesses, and increased government intervention in the market. This kind of interference stifles entrepreneurship and discourages investment, creating an environment where personal economic growth becomes difficult if not impossible.

Moreover, the emphasis on sustainability in the 2030 Agenda might also bring about economic regulation that could hamper personal ownership and economic freedom. Stricter environmental laws and regulations could limit the use of personal property, dictate how businesses operate, and enforce stringent measures on energy usage. While these initiatives aim to protect the planet, they can also further restrict economic activities and individual choices.

The move towards digital currencies controlled by central banks, as addressed earlier, further exacerbates the threat to economic freedom. Central Bank Digital Currencies (CBDCs) allow for unprecedented surveillance and control over individual transactions. Governments could potentially have the power to freeze accounts, track all monetary activity, and dictate how and where money should be spent. This level of control is alarming and brings into question the ability of individuals to freely manage their economic resources.

In tandem with the development of CBDCs is the rise of social credit systems. These score-based systems hold the capability to restrict economic actions based on one's behavior or compliance with state mandates. In a world where a low social credit score can result in denied financial services, restricted travel, and other economic sanctions, personal ownership and economic freedom become significantly compromised.

Another emerging threat is the growing emphasis on digital identities tied to economic transactions. While these IDs aim to improve security and streamline services, they could easily be repurposed to limit access to financial services based on a host of criteria, potentially extending to political, social, or even environmental behaviors. The loss of anonymity in transactions fundamentally alters how personal freedom can be exercised in the economic realm.

Furthermore, the role of multinational corporations in this landscape cannot be understated. As companies become increasingly integrated into the global governance mechanisms outlined by the 2030 Agenda, their business practices and policies might align more closely with these regulations. This could result in the corporate sector acting as enforcers of policies that erode economic freedom, whether through compliance with global tax codes, labor laws, or environmental regulations that stifle competition and innovation.

It is also essential to consider the educational systems and how future generations will be indoctrinated into accepting these changes. Educational reforms that emphasize collective over individual ownership could shape the mindset of the youth, making them more amenable to centralized economic controls. This indoctrination works against the fostering of entrepreneurial spirit and the aspiration to personal financial success, feeding into a cycle that sustains economic dependency on larger entities rather than individual agency.

There is a distinct peril in the potential for creeping governmental overreach. With increased regulation and oversight comes the danger of bureaucratic inefficiencies and corruption. Overburdened regulatory frameworks often lead to reduced economic dynamism, where smaller players find it exceedingly difficult to compete or even survive. Such an environment disproportionately affects small businesses and individual entrepreneurs, who are the backbone of economic freedom and innovation.

Lastly, public perception driven by media narratives also plays a crucial role. Media outlets framing economic policy debates in favor of the 2030 Agenda may suppress dissenting opinions and reduce critical scrutiny. This shapes public opinion in ways that make harmful policies more palatable, accelerating their implementation and entrenchment in the socio-economic fabric.

The combined weight of these threats creates a compelling case for vigilance and resistance. Preserving economic freedom requires understanding and confronting these dangers. Stakeholders—from policymakers to individual citizens—must rally together to protect the principles of personal ownership and economic liberty, ensuring that the march toward 2030 doesn't trample on our fundamental freedoms.

Chapter 15:
Impacts on Small Businesses
and Entrepreneurs

Small businesses and entrepreneurs represent the lifeblood of a thriving economy, driving innovation and creating jobs. However, the 2030 agenda presents legislative and regulatory shifts that could profoundly impact these vital sectors. One of the most significant changes is the increased regulation around environmental sustainability and labor practices. While intended to promote global good, these regulations could place an overwhelming burden on small businesses.

For many entrepreneurs, compliance with these new regulations requires significant financial investment. Consider the case of a small manufacturing business. Suddenly, they are required to upgrade their entire production process to meet stringent environmental criteria. Larger corporations may navigate these challenges with relative ease; however, smaller operations find themselves grappling with costs that could put them out of business.

One of the key aspects of the 2030 agenda is the push towards digital transformation. On the surface, this sounds beneficial. Yet, for small businesses less technologically savvy, the push to adopt complex digital infrastructure becomes a daunting challenge. Think of local mom-and-pop shops that now have to integrate sophisticated e-commerce platforms. This includes everything from digital IDs to cashless payment systems, all while trying to preserve a personal touch that attracts loyal customers.

The pandemic has already revealed vulnerabilities; many small enterprises lacked the resources to shift quickly to online operations. The accelerated pace of digital change mandated by the 2030 agenda could exacerbate these vulnerabilities, widening the gap between small businesses and large corporations that have the capital to invest in state-of-the-art technology.

Another area of concern is the potential stifling of innovation. Entrepreneurs are known for their disruptive ideas and willingness to take risks. However, increased surveillance and data-sharing requirements could deter innovative thinkers. Privacy concerns and stringent regulatory oversight might limit the freewheeling environment essential for groundbreaking innovations.

Economic concentration is a possible long-term implication. As small businesses struggle to comply with the new norms, many may close their doors permanently. This paves the way for larger corporations to monopolize various sectors. Consequently, consumer choice will diminish, and prices might soar due to the lack of competition. The individual entrepreneur, who once stood as a symbol of economic dynamism, risks becoming an endangered species under this new regime.

Few real-world examples illustrate these fears better than the food and beverage industry. A small café owner, bound by stringent food safety regulations and environmental standards, finds it nearly impossible to compete against large chains that bulk-buy resources and streamline operations across multiple locations. The result is a landscape where only the most resourceful or financially robust can thrive, often at the expense of diversity and local flavor.

Finally, the long-term economic impact cannot be understated. Small businesses contribute significantly to employment, especially at the local level. As these businesses collapse, unemployment rates could rise, leading to broader social and economic instability. The prosperity and innovation brought by local entrepreneurs are difficult to replace with homogenous, centralized systems of management and control.

In summary, while the 2030 agenda's goals might seem well-intentioned, their implementation could bring more harm than good to small businesses and entrepreneurs. The very fabric of local economies could be unalterably changed, shifting from diverse, vibrant hubs of activity to monolithic structures dominated by a few key players. The implications are both immediate and long-lasting, warranting careful consideration and advocacy for measures that preserve the entrepreneurial spirit.

Case Studies

The impacts of the 2030 Agenda on small businesses and entrepreneurs are far-reaching, yet underreported. In our examination, various case studies bring to light the practical and often harsh realities faced by these vital segments of our economy. From local mom-and-pop shops to tech start-ups, the agenda's wide-ranging policies pose both direct and ripple effects that are reshaping the entrepreneurial landscape.

Consider the story of Susan, who owns a small bakery in a mid-sized American town. Her business was already operating on thin margins when the 2030 Agenda introduced new environmental regulations aimed at reducing carbon footprints. While well-intentioned, these regulations translated to expensive equipment upgrades and rigorous compliance checks. For Susan, this meant either investing in costly new ovens that meet stringent emissions standards or facing hefty fines and potential shutdowns. Her choices were limited, putting immense financial strain on her once-thriving bakery.

Then there's the tech start-up founded by two college friends, Mark and Lisa. Initially, their innovative water purification technology attracted significant interest and venture capital. However, as the 2030 Agenda's digital and regulatory frameworks tightened, data privacy laws became more complex. Mark and Lisa found themselves spending more time and money navigating compliance landscapes than on innovation. This not only drained their initial capital but also hampered their growth prospects, causing them to lose a competitive edge in an already crowded market.

In another example, Juan operates a family-owned farming business that has been running for generations. New sustainable agriculture mandates required him to adopt practices that significantly altered his traditional farming methods. While these changes promised long-term environmental benefits, the short-term costs were insurmountable for Juan. He needed to invest in new technology and undergo training sessions, all while maintaining his current production levels to keep the business afloat. The financial burden forced him to take out loans, putting him at risk of eventual insolvency.

Similarly, entrepreneurs like Tom, who started an online retail business, are also finding themselves at a crossroads. The increasing focus on digital IDs and surveillance mechanisms meant he had to integrate complex authentication systems into his e-commerce platform. This requirement strained his resources and made his customer base uneasy about privacy, leading to decreased sales. Furthermore, his dependency on larger tech platforms for business operations exposed him to the risk of sudden policy changes, dictated by entities adhering strictly to the Agenda's guidelines.

Another compelling story is that of Aisha, who started a renewable energy consultancy firm. Despite her alignment with the 2030

Agenda's sustainability goals, she faced intense competition from well-funded multinational corporations. These larger entities had the advantage of accessing subsidies and incentives more easily, whereas Aisha found herself entangled in bureaucratic red tape. The uneven playing field made it challenging for her to scale her operations and secure long-term contracts.

The case of Raj, an entrepreneur in the healthcare sector, is equally revealing. His start-up, which focuses on affordable telehealth services, seemed to be in perfect alignment with the 2030 Agenda's aims for accessible healthcare. However, data security regulations and compliance costs soared, demanding hefty investment in cybersecurity measures. Raj discovered that maintaining service integrity while complying with these regulations was a balancing act that drained both his financial and human resources.

These case studies illuminate a disturbing trend: the 2030 Agenda, despite its noble objectives, often neglects the viability of small businesses and entrepreneurs. The additional regulatory burdens, financial pressures, and competitive disadvantages pose existential threats to these enterprises, essential cogs in the economic machinery.

Moreover, as governments push for centralized digital currencies and enhanced surveillance, small businesses find themselves under constant scrutiny. The world of commerce yearns for agility and adaptability, qualities inherently more pronounced in smaller enterprises. Enforcing rigid systems and uniformity stifles innovation and places unwarranted pressure on these businesses to conform or perish.

The cumulative impact is clear: a business environment where small businesses and entrepreneurs struggle to survive, let alone thrive. This shift does not merely affect individual entrepreneurs or small business owners. It reverberates throughout local communities, hollowing out main streets, disrupting local economies, and reducing consumer choices. Over time, these effects could erode the social and economic fabric that supports a diverse and vibrant market.

Consider the broader implications for employment. Small businesses are crucial job creators. Susan's bakery, Mark and Lisa's tech start-up, Juan's farm, Tom's online retail shop, Aisha's consultancy, and Raj's telehealth service collectively employ dozens of individuals. As these enterprises wobble under the weight of new regulations, job losses become inevitable. The transition from entrepreneurial enterprises to monopolistic conglomerates exacerbates unemployment, leading to socio-economic disenfranchisement.

Despite these challenges, the human spirit's resilience often shines through adversity. Many small business owners and entrepreneurs are devising innovative ways to navigate these turbulent waters. For example, some are pooling resources to meet compliance requirements collectively, leveraging shared services to reduce individual financial burdens. Others are pivoting their business models, exploring new markets, and adopting cutting-edge technologies to stay competitive.

These case studies serve as a stark reminder of the 2030 Agenda's unintended consequences on small businesses and entrepreneurs. While aiming for a more sustainable and equitable world, the balance between regulation and innovation must be carefully navigated. Recognizing and addressing these challenges is crucial for ensuring that small businesses not only survive but also flourish in a future shaped by global governance initiatives.

Long-term Economic Impact

The long-term economic impact on small businesses and entrepreneurs under the 2030 Agenda cannot be overstated. As larger corporate entities increasingly align themselves with the mandated sustainability goals, small businesses could find themselves at a severe disadvantage. The cascading effects of regulatory compliance, altered market dynamics, and changing consumer expectations will pose unprecedented challenges.

Initially, many small businesses might struggle with the evolving regulatory landscape. Compliance with new sustainability standards often requires substantial investment in processes, technology, and supply chains. While large corporations may have the resources to adapt, smaller enterprises frequently operate on thinner margins, making these investments more burdensome. Without the ability to scale or innovate as quickly, small businesses may be squeezed out of the market.

Entrepreneurs, often characterized by their agility and adaptability, might encounter barriers unseen before. The push towards meeting global sustainability benchmarks can stifle creativity with an overemphasis on compliance versus innovation. For instance, the cost of integrating eco-friendly materials or processes into their business models can be prohibitive for startups still in their nascent stages. This could lead to a decline in the number of new businesses formed, as the financial risks become too high.

The shift towards a digital economy, exacerbated by the 2030 Agenda, brings both opportunities and pitfalls. On one hand, digital platforms can provide small businesses with access to a global market. Yet, these same platforms are often dominated by tech giants, leaving little room for smaller players. Moreover, the increasing need for advanced cybersecurity measures to protect customer data—a priority under the digital ID and privacy tenets of the agenda—adds yet another layer of cost and complexity.

Small businesses reliant on traditional models or those less versed in technology may find it hard to survive in this increasingly digital-first world. The uneven access to digital infrastructure and education widens the gap between tech-savvy entrepreneurs and those left behind, potentially exacerbating economic inequalities within the entrepreneurial ecosystem.

Additionally, the promotion of the circular economy—a core principle of the 2030 Agenda—may necessitate a complete redesign of product life cycles and business operations. While this shift is well-intentioned, aimed at reducing waste and promoting sustainability, it inadvertently places significant pressure on small businesses and startups. The feasibility of transitioning to a circular model without substantial capital is questionable for many small enterprises, who may lack both the financial and intellectual resources to implement such changes.

Long-term, there is a growing concern that the homogenization driven by these global standards could stifle the diverse and innovative nature of small businesses. Each small enterprise brings a unique value proposition, catering to niche markets and localized needs. The rightful emphasis on global sustainability could lead to a one-size-fits-all approach, eroding this diversity and leading to a more monotonous business landscape dominated by large, compliant corporations.

Moreover, the emphasis on environmental, social, and governance (ESG) criteria, while beneficial for the planet and society at large, introduces another layer of complexity. Small businesses, often lean in structure, may not have dedicated resources to implement comprehensive ESG strategies. The cost of hiring consultants or diverting time and resources to these initiatives could detract from their core operational priorities. As a result, many small businesses may find themselves excluded from lucrative partnerships and funding opportunities that prioritize ESG compliance.

In regions where government policies are more aggressively aligned with the 2030 Agenda, small businesses might confront additional hurdles. Subsidies and incentives might be disproportionately allocated to larger entities better able to meet sustainability metrics. This creates an uneven playing field, where small businesses struggle to compete not only in terms of market dynamics but also in securing governmental support.

Entrepreneurs in sectors traditionally seen as antagonistic to sustainability, such as fossil fuels or heavy industry, face an existential threat. Transitioning to greener alternatives is not merely a strategic pivot; it could fundamentally alter the business model. For many, the necessary investment in research and development to innovate within these parameters is beyond their reach, possibly leading to business closures and job losses.

On a more positive note, the long-term economic landscape isn't entirely bleak for small businesses under the 2030 Agenda. Opportunities will arise in the form of new markets dedicated to sustainability—green technologies, renewable energy, recycling, and waste management. Entrepreneurs who can innovate within these fields might not only survive but thrive. The key lies in the ability to anticipate these trends and be nimble in planning and execution.

Micro-financing and supportive policies geared specifically towards small businesses could also mitigate some negative impacts. Governments and international bodies might recognize the vital role of entrepreneurs in driving sustainable innovation and provide targeted resources to support them. Initiatives that offer training, financial backing, and market access can play a crucial role in leveling the playing field.

Finally, collaborations and coalitions among small businesses can serve as a powerful buffer. By banding together, these entities can share resources, knowledge, and strategies to navigate the regulatory and market challenges posed by the 2030 Agenda. Cooperative logistics, bulk purchasing of sustainable materials, and shared innovation hubs could help distribute the burden more evenly and foster collective growth.

The long-term economic impact on small businesses and entrepreneurs under the 2030 Agenda will be a complex tapestry of challenges and opportunities. The ability to adapt, innovate, and collaborate will determine their survival and success in this evolving global economic landscape. While the challenges are manifold, the potential for those who can navigate this brave new world remains promising.

Chapter 16:
Surveillance and Digital Tracking

The world of surveillance has evolved dramatically in recent years, accelerating with the growth of digital technology. Governments and private entities alike have leveraged advancements in data collection to monitor citizens on an unprecedented scale. What was once relegated to the realms of science fiction is now an everyday reality. But the question that looms large is: at what cost?

The extent of citizen surveillance today is staggering. With ubiquitous smartphone usage, GPS tracking, and surveillance cameras on nearly every corner, the capacity to observe and record human activity has never been greater. Governments argue that such measures enhance security and streamline administrative processes. However, these technologies present a stark threat to personal privacy and autonomy.

Consider the data collected by Internet Service Providers (ISPs), tech giants like Google and Facebook, and countless other digital platforms. They capture your browsing history, search queries, social media interactions, and even private messages. This data is stored, analyzed, and, more often than not, sold to third parties. The implications are daunting: every click, like, and online interaction is no longer private but part of a vast, traceable database.

Facial recognition technology has added another layer of intrusion. Widely deployed across airports, concert venues, and public spaces, this technology not only identifies individuals but also tracks their movements over time. It's a system that operates both overtly and covertly, often with little to no public oversight or consent. The potential for abuse is immense, especially when this data is in the hands of entities with questionable motives.

The rise of digital tracking has stirred significant debate about the balance between security and personal freedom. Proponents claim it's essential for national security, helping to prevent terrorism and crime. Yet, critics argue that the pendulum has swung too far, tipping towards a surveillance state where the notion of privacy is virtually extinct.

The consequences for privacy are severe and multifaceted. On an individual level, the pervasive monitoring fosters a climate of self-censorship. People may alter their behavior, suppress dissenting opinions, and avoid certain activities out of fear that they are being watched. This chilling effect stifles free speech and narrows the breadth of acceptable discourse.

Moreover, such extensive surveillance can have broader societal repercussions. There's the risk of power being consolidated in the hands of a few, where data is weaponized to manipulate and control populations. Already, instances of digital surveillance have been linked to biased law enforcement practices, disproportionately affecting marginalized communities.

Political dissenters and activists often find themselves at heightened risk. Governments with stringent surveillance mechanisms can quickly identify and quash opposition before it gains momentum. It's a sobering scenario, one where the fight for personal freedom and privacy becomes increasingly arduous.

At the core of these concerns is the erosion of trust. When citizens feel their every move is monitored, trust in government and institutions diminishes. This erosion can lead to societal fractures, breeding alienation and unrest. It's a vicious cycle where increased surveillance begets more distrust, fueling further surveillance in the name of maintaining order.

While the use of surveillance is often justified under the guise of safety and efficiency, it's critical to evaluate whether these benefits truly outweigh the profound loss of privacy. Are we willing to sacrifice our personal freedoms for an illusion of security? This question needs rigorous debate and informed scrutiny.

Protecting privacy in the digital age demands action on multiple fronts. Individuals must become literate in digital hygiene practices, such as using encryption tools and being discerning about the information they share online. Legal frameworks should evolve to safeguard citizen data more rigorously, with stringent oversight and transparent processes. Additionally, tech companies must be held accountable for their data practices, ensuring they prioritize user privacy over profit.

In conclusion, surveillance and digital tracking pose significant threats to personal freedoms and privacy. As we edge closer to the 2030 agenda, the potential for these technologies to infringe upon human rights grows. It's imperative to confront these challenges head-on, fostering a discourse that seeks to protect individual freedoms while navigating the complexities of a digitally interconnected world.

Extent of Citizen Surveillance

In today's hyper-connected world, surveillance extends far beyond traditional cameras on street corners. Governments now possess unprecedented capabilities to monitor their citizens in myriad covert ways. The introduction of advanced digital tracking technologies has fundamentally altered the landscape of personal privacy, inching us closer to an age where every action is potentially scrutinized.

Modern surveillance isn't just limited to the physical world. Your smartphone, computer, and even smart home devices now double as sophisticated monitoring tools. Every email you send, every call you make, and even the websites you visit can be tracked and logged. Companies that provide these technologies argue they're enhancing user experience and safety. However, it's essential to ask: at what cost?

Metadata collection allows for an extraordinarily detailed overview of an individual's life. It's no longer a simple binary of "they know or they don't." Instead, a detailed mosaic of one's activities, preferences, and even ideological leanings can be constructed. This information can be, and often is, shared with government entities. Often without our explicit consent.

Facial recognition technology is another key player in the vast machinery of citizen surveillance. This technology has become increasingly sophisticated and its implementation widespread. What started as an experimental capability in airports or high-security areas has permeated public spaces, retail stores, and even schools. The constant monitoring raises crucial questions about consent and personal freedom. Are we exchanging our privacy for the illusion of security?

Governments often justify these invasive measures by citing national security and crime prevention. It's a compelling argument—who wouldn't want a safer society? But this reasoning often serves as a thin veil covering the troubling reality of pervasive citizen monitoring. Disputing the narrative becomes increasingly difficult as the surveillance infrastructure hardens, becoming a normalized aspect of modern life.

Surveillance extends into our online interactions as well. Social media platforms, search engines, and e-commerce sites harvest vast amounts of data. This data collection often happens with alarmingly little oversight, funneled into complex algorithms that predict our behavior with unsettling accuracy. These digital footsteps constitute a treasure trove of information that various actors, including governments, can exploit. The lines between corporate data mining and government surveillance blur, creating a disturbing partnership.

The most insidious aspect of modern surveillance might be its obscured nature. Unlike traditional surveillance methods, digital tracking is nearly invisible. This absence of a tangible, observable entity monitoring us makes it easier to forget or ignore. It's easy to discount the seriousness of the issue when you can't physically see it occurring, but make no mistake, it's ever-present.

Moreover, the scope of this surveillance is global. From democratic nations to authoritarian regimes, the use of digital tools to monitor populations has become a universal strategy. Technologies initially developed in one part of the world often find their way into the hands of less scrupulous governments. International cooperation and data sharing agreements further complicate the web of surveillance, blurring jurisdictional lines and making accountability nearly impossible.

Let's not forget the role of public-private partnerships in this grand scheme. Many governments rely on private technology firms to provide the infrastructure necessary for these surveillance operations. This relationship often benefits both parties—the government gets access to cutting-edge technology, while companies gain lucrative contracts and influence. However, the citizen's privacy is the sacrificial lamb in this arrangement.

Another key component to consider is legislative oversight—or the lack thereof. In many countries, laws governing surveillance have not kept pace with technological advancements. Vague and outdated statutes allow for broad interpretation and enforcement. This legal lag creates fertile ground for abuses of power, with citizens often left unaware of how closely they're being monitored or what recourses are available to them.

The concern reaches a different level when we consider the implementation of social credit systems in countries like China. While more detailed discussion of China's model is reserved for another section, it's imperative to acknowledge how such systems represent the apex of surveillance capabilities. They offer a stark glimpse into the potential future of citizen monitoring, making it crucial to contemplate these aspects when evaluating the extent of surveillance globally.

So, what can be done about this intricate web of surveillance tightening around us? Public awareness is the first step. Knowledge empowers people to demand greater transparency and accountability. Grassroots activism, legal challenges, and advocating for updated legislation can put pressure on both governments and corporations to respect privacy rights. It's also essential to support technologies and platforms that prioritize user privacy, sending a market signal that ethical practices matter to consumers.

In summation, the extent of citizen surveillance is both vast and complex. It encompasses a range of technologies, platforms, and behaviors designed to monitor our every move. While the promise of safety and convenience is tantalizing, it's imperative to remain vigilant. The cost of unchecked surveillance could very well be the erosion of essential freedoms that form the bedrock of democratic societies. Navigating this terrain requires both awareness and action, ensuring that our privacy isn't the ultimate price we pay for modern conveniences.

Consequences for Privacy

The encroaching presence of surveillance and digital tracking casts a long shadow over individual privacy. In an age where every click, purchase, and conversation can be monitored, the ramifications for personal freedom and privacy are profound. The scale of surveillance today is unprecedented, and it goes well beyond traditional government oversight. It involves corporate entities, international organizations, and even foreign governments.

First, we need to examine the data collection methods and their reach. From smartphones to smart appliances, we're surrounded by devices that collect vast amounts of data. This data isn't limited to visible activities like web searches or social media interactions. It extends to location data, biometric information, and even behavioral patterns. The cumulative effect of this data collection builds a comprehensive profile of individuals, often without their explicit consent.

Consider the implications of such detailed profiling. Companies can predict behaviors, preferences, and even future actions. While the convenient personalization of services sounds beneficial, it comes at the cost of reducing an individual to a set of data points. The more concerning issue is the potential misuse of this information. Examples range from micro-targeted political ads to identity theft. Even more unsettling is the prospect of this data falling into the hands of malicious actors.

Privacy erosion due to surveillance and digital tracking also affects social behavior. Knowing that one's actions are perpetually under scrutiny can lead to self-censorship. Surveillance can alter how we communicate, where we go, and how we express ourselves both online and offline. The chilling effect isn't just theoretical; it has real-world implications on freedom of speech and association. Individuals may avoid discussing sensitive topics or participating in public protests, fearing potential repercussions.

On a larger scale, societal norms about privacy are shifting. Younger generations, growing up in an era of constant connectivity, might view intrusive data collection as a given. The normalization of surveillance breeds complacency, making it harder to advocate for privacy rights. This shift also creates challenges for those who strive to maintain privacy. Opting out of data collection often means forfeiting conveniences and services, creating a dilemma: choose between privacy or modern convenience.

The framework that supports surveillance and digital tracking is often opaque. Laws and regulations vary widely among countries, lacking the consistency needed to enforce robust privacy protections globally. Moreover, legislative bodies struggle to keep pace with rapid technological advancements, resulting in outdated or insufficient regulations. This gray area allows both governments and corporations to expand their surveillance capabilities under dubious legal justifications.

Economic dependence on digital technologies also plays a crucial role. Many businesses argue that data collection is essential for service improvements and economic growth. While this has some truth, it overlooks the deeper issue of consent. Often, individuals are coerced into accepting invasive terms of use because rejecting them isn't a viable option. Whether it's for employment or basic online interactions, the power imbalance leaves individuals with little to no control over their own data.

There are also geopolitical dimensions to consider. Surveillance doesn't stop at borders. Various governments engage in international espionage and data collection, compromising global privacy. Partnerships between tech giants and governments further muddy the waters. These collaborations blur the lines between commercial interests and state surveillance, making it difficult to pinpoint responsibility or enforce accountability.

The rise of predictive policing and its reliance on extensive data troves expands the reach of surveillance into public safety and law enforcement. While aimed at reducing crime, these practices often lead to racial profiling and civil liberties violations. The ethical implications are significant. Using algorithms to pre-emptively flag individuals based on historical data often means perpetuating existing biases within marginalized communities, leading to systemic discrimination.

Furthermore, the anonymity of whistleblowers and journalists is at risk. These individuals rely on privacy to expose corruption and hold powers to account. Increased surveillance impedes their ability to communicate securely, potentially discouraging acts of whistleblowing altogether. In the absence of privacy protections, uncovering institutional malfeasance becomes extraordinarily challenging.

Mitigating these consequences requires robust legal frameworks, technological safeguards, and public awareness. Advocacy for transparent regulatory processes and stringent data protection laws is essential. Additionally, technological solutions like end-to-end encryption and decentralized data storage can offer some protection. Public discourse around privacy issues must remain active and vigilant to counterbalance the normalization of surveillance.

In conclusion, the far-reaching consequences of surveillance and digital tracking threaten to erode personal privacy fundamentally. This erosion doesn't merely affect individual autonomy but alters the broader social fabric. Restoring and safeguarding privacy will require a concerted effort from lawmakers, technology developers, and the public. As we move further into the 21st century, the balance between convenience and privacy will remain one of the defining challenges of our time.

Chapter 17:
Education and Indoctrination

As the 2030 Agenda continues to unfold, its reach isn't just in the realm of politics or finance. The implications stretch deep into our education systems. Curricular changes are made under the guise of forward-thinking innovation. In classrooms across the globe, traditional subjects are being blended with new narratives that fit the framework of the agenda.

Take history lessons, for instance. Rather than exploring multifaceted perspectives, students might now be presented with a streamlined version of events that aligns with the desired global outlook. This isn't just about adding new material; it's also about omitting key details that could encourage critical thinking or skepticism.

The shift isn't confined to history. Science and social studies are also being retooled. Climate change, economic disparities, and social justice are certainly vital topics, but when they're taught within a tightly controlled narrative, the lines between education and indoctrination blur. Students may leave school with a sense of certainty that doesn't account for the complexities of real-world issues.

Long-term effects on youth are a growing concern. The generation educated under these principles might face challenges in questioning authority or seeking diverse perspectives. Rather than producing critical thinkers, this system risks creating individuals who accept information at face value. The consequences can be far-reaching, affecting innovation, governance, and civic engagement.

How do these changes impact teachers? Educators find themselves at a crossroads. They're expected to uphold the new curriculum, often under significant pressure from administrative bodies. This shift can stifle creative teaching methods and reduce opportunities for students to exercise their intellectual independence.

What about parents? In many cases, they grapple with understanding the full scope of these changes. While some recognize the indoctrination potential, others see the introduced topics as essential for modern education. The dichotomy often results in polarized communities, where dialogue is replaced by opposition.

The landscape of education under the 2030 Agenda raises fundamental questions about the role of schooling in developing free-thinking, informed citizens. The balance between education and indoctrination has never been more delicate, requiring vigilance and active participation from all stakeholders.

Curricular Changes

Education is the foundation upon which societies build their future, but the 2030 Agenda fundamentally alters the framework. One of the most significant changes pertains to curricular content. The new curriculum aims to create globally aware citizens, aligning educational systems worldwide. While sounding benevolent, this goal possesses an undercurrent that necessitates scrutiny. The emphasis is no longer on national history, local culture, or independent critical thinking, but rather on a standardized global perspective.

Imagine classrooms where traditional subjects are supplemented, and often supplanted, by content that feeds into a globalist narrative. Subjects such as national history and government might see less focus, replaced by units on global citizenship and sustainable development. The idea is to cultivate a generation that sees the world not through the lens of national identity, but through a homogenized global prism.

A shift in curricular focus extends to environmental education as well. While raising awareness about environmental issues is undoubtedly important, the 2030 curriculum seeks to embed principles of sustainability into almost every subject. From math problems contextualized with carbon footprints to literature classes discussing climate refugees, it subtly alters perceptions and priorities toward a singular narrative: sustainability at all costs. Such pervasive messaging can steer students' beliefs and values, shaping them into compliant proponents of these ideals rather than independent thinkers.

Another notable component is the promotion of digital literacy. Initially, increasing comfort with technology appears advantageous. However, within the 2030 framework, this education often emphasizes monitoring systems, digital ID protocols, and online behavioral expectations. Far from fostering tech-savvy freedom, it can condition young minds to accept, even welcome, extensive digital oversight.

The curricular alterations also extend to social studies and civics. New content modules, often mandated by international bodies, focus on the interconnectedness of the world. Concepts like global governance, shared resources, and international regulations occupy significant classtime. While understanding global systems is important, the curriculum's slant might downplay the value of national sovereignty and self-governance.

STEM subjects aren't exempt from this wave of changes either. Science classrooms may incorporate heavy elements of climate science, often taught in a manner that brooks little debate. While acknowledging climate change is important, the lack of balanced teaching can marginalize skepticism, reducing complex issues to binary conclusions. Mathematics might see an infusion of statistical data from global reports, embedding a subconscious acceptance of global monitoring organizations' metrics.

The introduction of emotional and social learning (SEL) also raises eyebrows. Intended to develop empathy and emotional intelligence, the SEL curriculum under the 2030 agenda often emphasizes collective well-being over individual achievement. It aims to foster a sense of community and interconnectedness but could inadvertently devalue personal responsibility and individual accomplishment, reorienting youth to think more about the collective than themselves.

Humanities subjects undergo a transformation as well. Literature classes may prioritize works that highlight social justice issues, marginalized voices, and global challenges. While these stories are undoubtedly important, an overemphasis can narrow the literary canon and sideline classic and national literatures, altering the cultural touchstones for the next generation.

In higher education, these curricular shifts can affect academic freedom. Universities tied to international funding or partnerships may feel pressure to align their courses with 2030 agenda ideals. Research priorities could be influenced, guiding scholars toward topics that support sustainable development, global health, or similar themes over others. Over time, these shifts not only shape what is studied but what is valued in academic circles.

The practical implications of these curricular changes are profound. Students brought up in this educational milieu might emerge with a homogenized worldview, less appreciative of individual liberty or national borders. Critical thinking could take a backseat to rote acceptance of prescribed narratives. With young people molded into global citizens, willing to surrender personal freedoms for the perceived greater good, the seeds of future governance are sown in today's classrooms.

This reformed curriculum, while seemingly inclusive and forward-thinking, may be building a compliant and malleable society. It aims at a future where the lines between local and global blur, where individualism fades in favor of collectivism. The reduction in national historical studies, along with the focus on global wellness over individual accomplishment, fosters a generation less likely to question overarching authorities or challenge established global norms.

In summary, the curricular changes proposed by the 2030 Agenda go beyond simple updates in educational content. They signify a deeper, more insidious shift aimed at shaping young minds to fit a global template. By understanding these subtle yet powerful changes, one can better grasp the extent to which education is being used as a tool for global indoctrination. The consequences of such a transformation will echo far beyond the classrooms, shaping societies and governance structures in ways that might not be immediately visible but are certainly profound.

Long-term Effects on Youth

As we delve into the long-term effects on youth, it's essential to understand how the initiatives of the 2030 Agenda weave into the fabric of education and indoctrination. Shifts in curricular frameworks may seem benign at first glance, but they harbor changes that ripple into the psyche of future generations. How children are taught today will shape the way they perceive the world and interact with it. The curriculum is not merely a collection of subjects; it's the lens through which young individuals learn to view society, governance, and their roles within these constructs.

One significant consequence of these curricular changes is the potential erosion of critical thinking skills. When educational systems emphasize specific ideologies, there is a tendency to present information in a way that leaves little room for questioning. Subjects like history, economics, and social studies could be tailored to reflect the goals and visions of those driving the 2030 Agenda, encouraging conformity over exploration. This narrow framing can undermine a student's ability to think independently and critically assess diverse perspectives.

Moreover, there is a growing emphasis on global citizenship within the curriculum, which, while promoting a sense of unity, can dilute national identity. Young people may grow up with a skewed understanding of patriotism and the importance of national sovereignty. This shift can influence how future generations prioritize global issues over local or national concerns, potentially leading to a populace more susceptible to endorsing international policies over domestic interests.

It's also worthwhile to consider the psychological impact of such education. A child who is taught that their primary identity is as a global citizen may experience a form of cognitive dissonance when their personal or familial values clash with these global ideals. This could foster an internal conflict that impacts mental health, leading to increased anxiety, a diminished sense of self, and an overall feeling of disconnection from their immediate community.

Not only does this paradigm affect mental frameworks, but it also has tangible implications for youths' future career paths. As the agenda promotes specific sustainable development goals, educational systems may prioritize fields aligned with these goals. While this can drive innovation in areas like renewable energy and sustainable agriculture, it might inadvertently devalue traditional fields or industries deemed less critical to the global agenda. In doing so, students may feel pressured to pursue careers that are politically correct rather than those aligned with their personal interests and strengths.

Furthermore, the integration of digital IDs and increased surveillance within educational institutions introduces another layer of complexity. The collection and monitoring of student data might be justified under the guise of personalization and security; however, it stands as a tool for control. Students grow up in an environment where they are constantly monitored, potentially normalizing a future where privacy is a luxury rather than a right. This normalization could stifle creativity and innovation, for fear of stepping outside the accepted norms.

The implementation of a social credit system, similar to what we see in places like China, is another alarming prospect. If adopted globally, such a system could start impacting students from a young age. Behavior in school, extracurricular activities, and even social interactions could feed into a score that influences future opportunities. The conformity necessary to maintain a high score might suppress individuality and discourage risk-taking, both of which are crucial for personal development and innovation.

Moreover, the psychological impact of growing up under a social credit system can't be ignored. Constant surveillance and evaluation might create a generation of individuals more focused on maintaining an acceptable public persona rather than developing authentic relationships and genuine self-expression. This could lead to a society rife with superficial interactions, where trust and loyalty become rare commodities.

Beyond personal development, there are implications for civic engagement. Youth taught to comply and conform are less likely to challenge the status quo, potentially leading to a more passive citizenry. This dynamic can have far-reaching implications for democratic processes. If future generations are less engaged and less willing to question authority, the fundamental principles of a free society could erode over time. Centralized power could solidify, leaving little room for grassroots movements and local governance initiatives.

The education system's role in shaping societal values is profound and cannot be underestimated. It's not just about what is being taught, but how it's being taught and for what purpose. When education serves as a vehicle for indoctrination rather than enlightenment, the effects on youth are inevitable and enduring. A society's values shift from critical thought to blind acceptance, from individualism to collectivism, and from questioning authority to unwavering compliance.

It's critical for us to monitor the changes within educational frameworks closely and to understand their broader implications. Do these changes serve the purpose of creating informed, engaged citizens, or are they stepping stones to a more controlled global society? The future lies in the balance, shaped by the education and indoctrination of today's youth. Our vigilance now is paramount to ensuring that the values of freedom, critical thought, and individuality are preserved for generations to come.

Chapter 18:
Political Influence and Lobbying

Political influence and lobbying are integral to understanding the behind-the-scenes mechanisms that drive the 2030 Agenda. Although these efforts often operate outside public scrutiny, they are critical in shaping policies and aligning governmental priorities with specific agendas. Therefore, examining the role that influential figures and lobbying efforts play is crucial for anyone aiming to grasp the full scope of the 2030 Agenda.

Various key influencers shape the political landscape in the context of the 2030 Agenda. These figures are not limited to elected officials but extend to business magnates, heads of international organizations, and even public intellectuals. Their influence can be attributed to their control over vast resources, networks of connections, or the fear of retribution. These individuals wield substantial power in directing conversations and shaping policy outcomes.

How do these influencers achieve their goals? A primary method is through lobbying. Lobbying involves the concerted efforts to sway legislators, regulators, and public opinion to favor particular objectives. This process is far from transparent; it often takes place in private meetings, at exclusive events, or through intricate networks of intermediaries. By providing financial incentives, promises of future assistance, or leveraging their social capital, these influencers successfully alter the trajectory of legislation and public policy.

To illustrate, consider how climate policies often align closely with the interests of multinational corporations. While these companies publicly advocate for sustainable practices, they simultaneously lobby for regulations that benefit them financially. This duality demonstrates how lobbying can create an appearance of ethical governance while shielding underlying profit-driven motivations.

Beyond corporate interests, non-governmental organizations (NGOs) and international bodies like the United Nations play significant roles. These entities often have considerable sway in national governments through advocacy and lobbying. They engage in campaigns, fund research, and harness media platforms to push their agenda. This isn't to say that all their efforts are malicious; some genuinely aim for global betterment. However, the potential for hidden objectives always exists, requiring scrutiny.

The policy-shaping process is another critical area influenced by lobbying. Special interest groups and advocates draft policy recommendations well before they reach legislative bodies. These drafts often contain technical language and proposals that legislators may not fully understand, leaving room for loopholes or unexamined clauses. Additionally, these policies frequently go through multiple iterations of review and amendment, influenced at every stage by lobbying efforts.

Moreover, election cycles present an opportune time for lobbyists and influencers to ramp up their activities. Campaign contributions from powerful donors often come with expectations, subtly ensuring that elected officials act in alignment with the donors' interests. As a result, policies that emerge during these periods may reflect the objectives of a select few rather than the populace at large.

Understanding the labyrinthine pathways of political influence and lobbying sheds light on the complexities of the 2030 Agenda. While many aspects of this agenda promise a brighter future, the means by which these policies are shaped can cast a long shadow. As such, audiences must remain vigilant, discerning, and critical of the forces steering global governance. The true impact of these influences extends far beyond what's visible on the surface, demanding continuous scrutiny and accountability.

Key Influencers

In the intricate maze of political influence and lobbying surrounding the 2030 agenda, key influencers are the puppeteers behind the curtain. These individuals and entities shape the discourse, direct policy decisions, and wield immense power in navigating the global political landscape. Among them, a select few have emerged as particularly impactful, driving the agenda with fervor and unparalleled authority.

Arguably, one of the most prominent figures in this arena is Klaus Schwab, founder and executive chairman of the World Economic Forum (WEF). Schwab's vision, encapsulated in the notion of the Great Reset, intersects seamlessly with many of the goals outlined in the 2030 agenda. By leveraging the annual Davos meetings, where the world's elite gather, Schwab has positioned himself as a central influencer in global policymaking, pushing forward ideas on digital transformation, sustainability, and economic restructuring.

Schwab's influence isn't confined to intellectual contributions alone. The WEF, under his leadership, actively engages with governments, corporations, and civil society organizations. This tripartite engagement model amplifies the reach and impact of Schwab's ideas, embedding them into various facets of governance and corporate strategies worldwide. As a result, policies inspired by WEF's frameworks often gain traction rapidly, fueled by the backing of powerful stakeholders from diverse sectors.

However, Schwab isn't the solitary force at play. Political leaders from influential nations also play critical roles, often acting as both advocates and executors of the 2030 agenda. In Canada, for instance, Prime Minister Justin Trudeau has been vocal about his support for the agenda, integrating its goals into national policy. Trudeau's government has implemented several initiatives in alignment with the agenda's objectives, particularly in areas like climate action and digital inclusion.

Likewise, figures from the United Nations, such as António Guterres, the Secretary-General, are pivotal in the agenda's propagation. Guterres has consistently highlighted the urgency of addressing global challenges through collective action, positioning the 2030 agenda as a comprehensive roadmap for achieving this. His speeches, reports, and interactions with global leaders underscore the critical nature of the agenda, aiming to garner widespread political commitment.

Private sector leaders also wield significant influence. CEOs of major corporations, particularly those in tech and finance, play dual roles as both implementers of the agenda's principles within their companies and as lobbyists for broader systemic changes. Sundar Pichai of Google, Tim Cook of Apple, and Satya Nadella of Microsoft exemplify this dual influence. Their firms' policies on digital innovation, data management, and sustainability set industry standards and often inform public policy.

An often-overlooked aspect of this influence web is the role of think tanks and non-governmental organizations (NGOs). Entities like the Brookings Institution, the Bill and Melinda Gates Foundation, and the Open Society Foundations contribute profoundly through research, funding, and advocacy. These organizations shape policy by providing empirical evidence, proposing actionable recommendations, and mobilizing public opinion around key issues within the 2030 agenda.

Consider the philanthropic efforts of Bill Gates. His foundation has directed substantial resources towards health initiatives, renewable energy, and digital education, aligning closely with several Sustainable Development Goals (SDGs). By fostering partnerships with governments and other NGOs, Gates amplifies the agenda's reach and effectiveness, making substantial progress in areas that might otherwise remain underfunded or neglected.

Lobbyists, on the other hand, are the connective tissue that binds these influencers to policymakers. Through strategic engagements, they ensure that the interests of these key figures are represented in legislative processes. This often involves a blend of direct lobbying, grassroots mobilization, and media campaigns, aimed at shaping public and political narratives to favor the adoption of 2030 agenda-aligned policies.

In the midst of these multifaceted influences, it's essential to acknowledge the interplay between global and local actors. While international figures set the stage for grand ambitions, local politicians and influencers adapt these to their specific contexts. This dynamic creates a layered, complex influence matrix where global directives meet local realities, resulting in varied degrees of agenda implementation and adaptation.

Moreover, the influence isn't always exerted transparently. Many key influencers operate behind the scenes, using their networks and financial power to drive specific outcomes. This opacity can often lead to skepticism and resistance among those who feel disenfranchised or threatened by the agenda's goals. The tension between transparency and strategic influence remains a contentious aspect, underscoring the need for a balanced, inclusive approach to global policymaking.

As we navigate through the coming chapters, we'll explore how these influences manifest in concrete policies and actions. From digital ID implementation to shifts in financial systems, the fingerprints of these key influencers are evident. Understanding their motivations, strategies, and impacts is crucial for discerning the broader implications of the 2030 agenda on personal freedoms and societal structures.

How Policies Are Shaped

Policymaking, a nuanced and complex process, is fundamentally shaped by a myriad of elements including political influence and lobbying. These forces, often operating behind closed doors, play a significant role in the formation and implementation of policies that align with broader agendas like the 2030 Agenda. Understanding the interplay between political actors and lobbyists is crucial to grasping how policies are crafted and pushed through legislative bodies.

One key mechanism through which policies are shaped is lobbying. Lobbyists, often well-connected and highly experienced, work tirelessly to promote certain agendas, sometimes in ways that aren't immediately apparent. They cultivate relationships with politicians, provide expertise, and ensure that their clients' interests are represented at various levels of government. Lobbying can take many forms: from direct meetings and consultations to more subtle efforts like drafting legislation or regulatory frameworks.

Political contributions also heavily influence policy formation. Politicians, running costly campaigns, often rely on donations from individuals and organizations. These contributions can lead to a reciprocal relationship where policymakers feel obliged to support the interests of their benefactors. This financial aspect is a potent tool for shaping policies that align with donors' ideologies and goals, sometimes at the expense of broader public interests.

Another critical factor in shaping policies is the formation of think tanks and advisory committees. These entities, usually funded by wealthy individuals or corporations, provide research and policy recommendations. While they are often portrayed as neutral and objective, the reality is their outputs frequently echo the preferences and interests of their sponsors. The recommendations made by these groups can significantly steer the direction of policy discussions and decisions.

Media influence shouldn't be overlooked either. Media outlets, including news organizations and social media platforms, can frame issues in ways that sway public opinion and, by extension, political action. Policymakers are acutely aware of the media landscape, and decisions are often influenced by the need to maintain a positive public image or to avoid controversy. Media campaigns, often orchestrated by lobbyists and influencers, can apply pressure to fast-track or hinder certain policies.

The personal beliefs and experiences of policymakers themselves also play a role. While external influences are significant, the internal convictions of politicians, shaped by their backgrounds and ideological leanings, affect the kinds of policies they advocate for and support. This subjective dimension adds another layer of complexity to the policy-shaping process.

Furthermore, intergovernmental organizations exert considerable influence. Institutions like the United Nations and the World Economic Forum have platforms that bring together policymakers from around the world. These meetings often set the agenda and establish frameworks that member nations adopt and implement. The 2030 Agenda, for instance, has been shaped by a series of global summits and agreements, influencing national and local policies worldwide.

Industry-specific lobbying efforts can't be ignored. Key sectors like finance, technology, healthcare, and energy have dedicated lobbying groups that work relentlessly to shape policies in their favor. These sectors have a substantial impact on economic and social policies, leveraging their resources and expertise to craft legislation that benefits them, often under the guise of public good.

Lastly, grassroots movements and public advocacy also contribute to how policies are shaped, though their impact is often more erratic and dependent on levels of public engagement and media coverage. While these movements can sometimes successfully pressure policymakers to act in the public's interest, their influence is often countered by the more consistent and resource-rich efforts of professional lobbyists and established political actors.

Understanding how policies are shaped requires an awareness of the multifaceted interactions between various actors and the motivations driving them. It's rarely a straightforward process and is often shrouded in a veil of complexity and, at times, secrecy. Recognizing these dynamics is essential for those who wish to see through the veneer of political rhetoric and appreciate the real forces at play in policy formation.

Chapter 19:
The Role of Big Tech

The influence of technology companies on the global stage has grown exponentially in recent years. Giants like Google, Amazon, Facebook, and Apple are not just companies; they are powerful entities shaping policy and public perception. Their involvement in the 2030 agenda is undeniable, as they possess the tools to gather vast amounts of data and influence behavior on a scale previously unimaginable.

One of the primary ways big tech companies exert their influence is through data harvesting. Every click, like, and share contributes to extensive profiles on individuals, which can then be sold or used in predictive analytics. This data is a goldmine for governments and corporations alike, providing insights into the population's preferences, behaviors, and even potential dissent. The commodification of personal data raises significant privacy concerns, especially when these insights are used to manipulate behavior or enforce compliance with specific agendas.

Moreover, big tech's monopoly over platforms for communication and commerce gives them disproportionate control over public discourse. Algorithms determine what content is promoted or suppressed, subtly shaping public opinion and curating the information that individuals are exposed to. This gatekeeping role has profound implications for democracy and freedom of speech. Critics argue that it creates echo chambers and filter bubbles, where dissenting opinions are marginalized and critical discussion is stifled.

In addition, the financial clout of these companies allows them to lobby for favorable policies and regulations. With resources that surpass those of many nation-states, big tech can influence legislation to protect and expand their interests. This often includes efforts to sidestep antitrust laws, avoid taxation, and ensure their pivotal role in the future's digital landscape. The ties between technology giants and policymakers are complex and far-reaching, ensuring that their vision aligns with the broader goals set forth in the 2030 agenda.

Some argue that this symbiotic relationship between big tech and governments is a double-edged sword. On one hand, technology can drive innovation and simplify complex challenges. On the other, unchecked power in the hands of a few tech behemoths can undermine democracy, reduce personal freedoms, and create a society where individuals are increasingly monitored and controlled.

As we move closer to 2030, the role of big tech will likely become even more pronounced. It is essential to scrutinize the alignment of these corporations with global governance goals and consider the implications for privacy, autonomy, and freedom. The potential for misuse of power is immense, and awareness and vigilance are crucial in ensuring that technological advancements benefit all, rather than a select few.

Influence of Technology Companies

Big Tech companies have ingrained themselves in every fabric of our modern lives. They wield an unprecedented level of influence, shaping not just markets but also public policy and individual behaviors. This section will delve into how these technology behemoths play a key role within the broader scope of the 2030 Agenda. We've seen them rise from humble beginnings to becoming the titans of industry, controlling vast amounts of data and, consequently, power.

The influence of technology companies extends beyond the development of new gadgets or innovative software. These corporations are intertwined with national governments and international bodies, including those spearheading the 2030 Agenda. Take, for example, their role in data collection and analytics. Social media giants and search engines store unfathomable amounts of personal data, which can be used to shape public opinion, influence elections, and control financial markets. The data harvested is not merely about user behavior online; it paints a detailed picture of each individual's preferences, habits, beliefs, and even vulnerabilities.

We also need to consider the financial clout that these firms possess. Their market capitalization often exceeds the GDPs of small to medium-sized countries, giving them immense leverage. This financial power allows them to lobby effectively for laws and regulations that align with their interests. The fact that these companies can influence policy-making processes raises questions about democracy, sovereignty, and who truly governs public spaces.

Moreover, technology companies are pivotal in the implementation of digital identification systems, which are an intrinsic part of the 2030 Agenda. Digital ID systems promise efficiency and security, but they also pose significant privacy risks. Imagine a world where every movement, transaction, and interaction is logged. While this might improve administrative efficiencies, it can also lead to a mass surveillance state. The potential for abuse is high, especially when the collected data can be sold, hacked, or misused by those in power.

Another troubling aspect is the monopolistic tendencies of these companies. Amazon dominates e-commerce, Google controls search, and Facebook governs social media interactions to a large extent. Such concentration of power can stifle competition and innovation, making it difficult for smaller players to thrive. When companies hold monopolies, they have less incentive to protect consumer rights, prioritize privacy, or foster free speech.

For policymakers collaborating on the 2030 Agenda, technology companies are both partners and challenges. On one hand, their technological advancement and infrastructure can provide essential tools for achieving sustainable development goals. On the other hand, their unchecked power can also derail efforts aimed at equitable governance and individual freedoms. This duality makes Big Tech a contentious stakeholder in global initiatives aimed at shaping the future.

Still, the ambition of these corporations rarely aligns with the ideals of transparency and accountability. The algorithms they develop are often described as opaque "black boxes," impenetrable to public scrutiny. Decisions made by artificial intelligence can have far-reaching consequences, yet the rationale behind these decisions is shielded by layers of proprietary secrecy. This lack of transparency becomes particularly concerning when algorithms are used for critical societal functions, from healthcare to criminal justice.

Corporate social responsibility (CSR) initiatives are another area where technology companies wield influence. While many of these companies publicly champion social causes, such as sustainability and human rights, there's often a disparity between their public stances and their internal practices. This form of "greenwashing" can distract from more substantive critiques and allow these companies to continue practices that might be harmful in the long run.

In conclusion, technology companies have carved out a monumental role in the political, social, and economic landscapes of our world. Their influence in the 2030 Agenda is undeniable, raising both opportunities and concerns. As we move forward, it's crucial to scrutinize the role these corporations play; demanding transparency, accountability, and ethical behavior will be essential in shaping a future that prioritizes individual freedoms and equitable development. Whether through data collection, financial muscle, or technological innovations, the footprint of Big Tech in our societal structures will only grow. Understanding this influence is the first step in navigating the complexities it introduces to our lives and the global agenda at large.

Data Harvesting and Usage

The role of Big Tech in the 2030 Agenda is a key element that can't be overlooked. Within this framework, data harvesting and its subsequent usage stand as pivotal topics of concern. In a world becoming increasingly dependent on digital technology, the collection and utilization of vast quantities of data affect virtually every aspect of our daily lives. It is not simply about storing information; it's about what this information is used for, and more critically, who controls it.

Big Tech companies such as Google, Facebook, and Amazon have grown far beyond simple service providers. They are now data giants, gathering information on an unprecedented scale. Every click, purchase, and interaction is meticulously recorded, processed, and often shared or sold to third parties. This data isn't just numbers and statistics—it's deeply personal. It contains our preferences, our routines, our very identities. The implications of this are staggering when seen through the lens of the 2030 Agenda.

One of the fundamental concerns rests with privacy. For most, the concept of privacy has always implied a certain level of anonymity, a domain for personal thoughts and actions away from the prying eyes of everyone else. Yet, with the current trajectory of data harvesting, privacy is becoming more of an illusion. Constantly being monitored and analyzed, every digital footprint we leave is being used to build comprehensive profiles that can predict behavior with alarming accuracy.

Data usage, especially in the hands of big tech companies, extends beyond mere marketing. It's employed in behavioral analysis, influencing political viewpoints, swaying elections, and even in social engineering. Algorithms decide what content we see on social media, effectively shaping our view of the world. Consider how recommendation systems guide our choices—whether it's the news articles we read, the products we buy, or even the friends we connect with online.

These vast data repositories aren't just valuable in the marketplace; they're of immense interest to governments and regulatory bodies. Under the 2030 Agenda, the blurring lines between corporate data assets and governmental oversight become even more concerning. The potential for misuse in surveillance, tracking, and monitoring citizens is not a distant dystopian scenario but a tangible, looming reality. National security interests and public safety are often cited as justifications for deeper and more invasive data scrutiny.

A practical example can be seen in China's approach to data harvesting. Utilizing a network of cameras, social media activity, and general online behavior, the Chinese government has implemented one of the most extensive surveillance systems in the world. Their social credit system exemplifies the dangers of combining big tech capabilities with governmental control, leading to severe consequences for personal freedoms.

The concentration of vast amounts of personal data within a few powerful companies raises another significant issue: centralization of power. With so much knowledge about individuals' lives, these tech giants wield enormous influence. They can, and do, leverage this data to set terms for organizations and even governments. This concentration of influence can undermine democratic processes and give disproportionate power to an unelected few, swaying not just markets but political outcomes as well.

Moreover, the mechanisms for accountability are woefully inadequate. As many governments either lack the expertise or the will to regulate these entities effectively, a significant portion of the control resides with the tech companies themselves. They often operate in opacity, masking how they use, share, or secure the data in their possession.

The potential for misuse extends beyond national borders, creating a global issue that requires global attention. The European Union's GDPR attempts to enforce stricter data protection rules, but even these measures fall short in addressing the overarching concern of centralized data control. Where policies are lax, these tech conglomerates thrive, navigating around existing laws to maximize their data-gathering capabilities.

Commonly, the collected data is used to refine algorithms and artificial intelligence, improving products and services. While this can lead to innovations and conveniences, the ethical considerations are less straightforward. The use of data to predict and influence actions borders on manipulation, eradicating the notion of free will in many decisions. How much of what we choose is genuinely our choice if algorithms are nudging us in predefined directions?

Furthermore, citizens often have little control over how their data is used, even with supposed consent mechanisms in place. The "terms and conditions" that we routinely accept without reading grant broad permissions, effectively signing away our privacy. Once our data is in the hands of these tech giants, reclaiming it or even understanding how it's being used becomes nearly impossible.

Data harvesting by Big Tech serves as the backbone of the 2030 Agenda's extensive control mechanisms. This isn't a cautionary tale for the distant future but a pressing issue of the present. As we move towards 2030, the power dynamics inherent in the control of data will only intensify. If left unchecked, these practices will profoundly reshape society, placing control over personal freedoms and societal structures in the hands of a select few technocrats.

Chapter 20:
Resistance Movements and Activism

As the 2030 Agenda unfolds, resistance movements and activism have emerged as powerful forces standing against its sweeping changes. These movements vary in size, scope, and influence but share a common goal: to preserve personal freedoms and counteract perceived overreach by global institutions. The activists involved are often driven by deep-seated beliefs in sovereignty, human rights, and democratic principles, seeing their efforts as both a moral and strategic necessity.

Key figures such as Edward Snowden and Julian Assange have become symbols of resistance, exposing governmental surveillance and sparking global debates on privacy and freedom. Their actions have inspired a new generation of whistleblowers and activists who see transparency and accountability as critical to curbing the expansive reach of international agendas. However, these figures also face significant challenges, including legal threats, imprisonment, and public vilification.

Groups like the Electronic Frontier Foundation (EFF), Fight for the Future, and Digital Rights Foundation have been at the forefront of advocating for digital privacy and combating intrusive surveillance technologies. These organizations employ a mix of legal action, public awareness campaigns, and direct advocacy to influence policy and protect individual rights. Although their successes are notable, they often find themselves up against well-funded governmental and corporate interests. Nevertheless, these groups persist, emphasizing the importance of digital privacy as a cornerstone of modern freedom.

In various countries, grassroots movements have arisen to challenge the centralization of power and advocate for local autonomy. For instance, the Yellow Vests in France began as a protest against fuel taxes but quickly evolved into a broader campaign against the perceived disconnect between the ruling elite and the general populace. These movements often highlight economic inequities, the erosion of national sovereignty, and the diminished role of public opinion in shaping policy.

Despite their shared goals, resistance movements face significant obstacles. The primary challenge lies in the varied and often fragmented nature of these groups. While some focus on digital privacy, others concentrate on economic freedoms, national sovereignty, or environmental concerns. This fragmentation can dilute their overall impact and make unified action more difficult. Additionally, governments and powerful entities have become increasingly adept at countering activism through propaganda, legal restrictions, and surveillance.

However, moments of success are not uncommon. The halting or modification of controversial policies can often be traced back to concerted activism. Examples include the successful opposition to the Stop Online Piracy Act (SOPA) in the United States and various grassroots victories in local regions that have pushed back against centralized control. The use of social media and digital platforms has also amplified the reach and impact of these movements, democratizing the flow of information and rallying global support.

Activists continuously adapt their strategies, learning from past mistakes and leveraging new technologies to resist surveillance and censorship. Encryption tools, secure communication channels, and decentralized platforms have become essential in organizing and executing resistance activities. These tools not only safeguard the identities of activists but also ensure that their message cuts through the noise generated by mainstream media channels.

As the 2030 Agenda progresses, the role of resistance movements will remain crucial. These groups serve as a check against potential overreach and abuse of power, reminding global institutions that the quest for progress must not come at the cost of individual freedoms. In the chapters that follow, we'll delve into the legal battles, international coalitions, and media narratives shaping this resistance, offering a comprehensive view of the multifaceted struggle against the 2030 Agenda.

Key Figures and Groups

The landscape of resistance against the 2030 Agenda is populated by a variety of key figures and groups. These entities operate on national, regional, and international levels, using their influence to push back against what they perceive as an overreach of global governance.

One prominent figure in this movement is Robert F. Kennedy Jr. Known for his environmental advocacy, Kennedy has increasingly turned his attention toward issues of personal freedom and autonomy. He argues that the 2030 Agenda represents a threat to individual liberties and has established several initiatives aimed at raising public awareness and mobilizing action. His speeches often highlight the dangers of centralization and loss of personal ownership, resonating with many who fear the encroachment of global powers on local governance.

Another notable figure is Naomi Wolf, an author and political consultant who has become a vocal critic of both digital identification systems and the broader implications of the 2030 Agenda. Wolf's work often explores the intersections of technology, privacy, and personal freedom, shedding light on how modern digital systems can be leveraged for control rather than empowerment. Her written works provide a comprehensive critique of these systems, driving home the point that the path to so-called global wellbeing might come at the expense of individual rights.

Among the groups taking a firm stand against the 2030 agenda is the World Council for Health (WCH). This coalition of health-focused organizations aims to promote evidence-based approaches to health and wellness, free from the influence of what they describe as the "pharmaceutical-industrial complex." They argue that the 2030 Agenda, with its emphasis on digital health passports and centralized healthcare systems, undermines medical freedoms. The WCH often collaborates with other organizations to host conferences and webinars, informing the public about the risks posed by these global health strategies.

The Citizens for Free Speech (CFFS) is another key group in this resistance movement. They focus on defending First Amendment rights in the face of increasing restrictions. Their activism is grounded in the belief that free speech is the linchpin of all other freedoms. CFFS conducts grassroots campaigns, workshops, and public education efforts to arm citizens with the knowledge and tools they need to resist governmental overreach. They underscore the idea that without the ability to speak freely, meaningful resistance becomes impossible.

The Council on National Policy (CNP) plays a quieter but equally significant role. Operating behind the scenes, this influential group of conservative leaders works to shape policy decisions and public opinion against the 2030 Agenda. Comprising politicians, business leaders, and activists, the CNP employs a strategic approach, leveraging their networks to influence legislation and support candidates who oppose globalist policies. Their approach is less about public demonstrations and more about targeted, high-level lobbying and advocacy.

Then there is the Open Rights Group (ORG), a civil liberties group dedicated to preserving privacy and freedom in the digital age. Their work includes campaigning against intrusive surveillance measures and advocating for robust data protection laws. They view the data-harvesting aspects of the 2030 Agenda as deeply problematic, arguing that such practices pave the way for invasive social credit systems reminiscent of China's model. The ORG organizes hackathons, legal challenges, and public awareness campaigns that inform citizens about the perils of unchecked data accumulation.

Internationally, groups like the International Coalition for Democratic Values (ICDV) have formed to oppose the global governance elements of the 2030 Agenda. This coalition comprises various countries' sovereignty movements, each unified by the belief that supranational organizations like the UN should not dictate national policies. The ICDV frequently organizes international conferences, bringing together thought leaders and activists to strategize and share best practices for resisting the agenda's imposition.

On a more localized scale, grassroots movements are sprouting up across various nations. In Canada, the Take Back Our Freedoms (TBOF) group advocates against perceived encroachments on personal liberties, ranging from pandemic restrictions to broader elements of the 2030 Agenda. They engage in local activism, community meetings, and dissemination of information to rally citizens in defense of their freedoms. Their work is characterized by a strong focus on educating the public and pushing for policy changes at the municipal and provincial levels.

It's important to highlight the role of independent journalists and media platforms in this resistance. Figures such as independent journalist Glenn Greenwald have become pivotal in exposing the intricacies of the 2030 Agenda. Through articles, interviews, and social media, these journalists provide detailed analyses and uncover aspects that mainstream outlets might overlook or downplay. Their work acts as a crucial counterbalance to dominant narratives, providing citizens with alternative perspectives.

Lastly, the rise of decentralized networks has empowered a new wave of digital activists. Utilizing platforms like blockchain and encrypted communication channels, these activists organize and mobilize without the risk of censorship. Groups like the Decentralized Autonomous Organization for Freedom (DAO-F) have leveraged decentralized technology to bypass traditional regulatory constraints, offering a glimpse into how technology can be reclaimed as a tool for resistance rather than control.

In summary, the resistance to the 2030 Agenda is multifaceted and dynamic. It spans prominent individuals, specialized coalitions, grassroots movements, and digital networks. Each of these actors brings unique strengths and perspectives to the fight, united by a shared commitment to preserving personal freedoms and local sovereignty. As the global push toward centralized governance continues, these key figures and groups will likely remain at the forefront, challenging the agenda every step of the way.

Successes and Challenges

Resistance movements against the 2030 Agenda have seen both remarkable wins and notable hurdles. In the battle to maintain personal freedoms and economic sovereignty, activists have employed a variety of strategies, from grassroots movements to legal challenges. These efforts have generated considerable attention and, in some cases, slowed or even reversed certain policy implementations.

One of the most prominent successes has been the ability of grassroots organizations to mobilize rapidly and create substantial awareness about the potential dangers posed by the 2030 Agenda. Social media has been an invaluable tool in this regard, allowing activists to spread their messages quickly and effectively. Protests and rallies have drawn large crowds, showcasing the population's growing concern about increased government control.

For instance, the widespread protests against digital ID initiatives have managed to halt the rollout in several regions. Activists leveraged data privacy concerns to galvanize public opinion, making it impossible for proponents to ignore the resistance. Their efforts have resonated particularly well in areas with a strong tradition of personal liberties, leading to significant policy reconsiderations.

Despite these victories, challenges abound. Firstly, the scale and influence of organizations behind the 2030 Agenda, such as the World Economic Forum and the United Nations, present a formidable opposition. These institutions have vast resources at their disposal, allowing them to counter-mobilize with aggressive PR campaigns and political lobbying. They can paint resistance groups as fringe entities or conspiracy theorists, undermining their credibility in the eyes of the broader public.

In terms of policy, resistance movements face a complex legislative landscape. Many nations have already begun implementing aspects of the 2030 Agenda in subtle ways that can be difficult to contest legally. For example, changes in environmental regulations and financial policies are often justified under the guise of sustainable development, making it challenging to argue against them without appearing to oppose environmental protection or economic reform.

Legal battles have yielded mixed results. While some court cases have resulted in the blocking of invasive digital tracking laws, others have fallen short due to the intricate nature of international regulations and the precedent of existing laws. The legal framework often lags behind technological advancements, making it a slow and arduous task to formulate effective legal arguments against digital surveillance and central bank digital currencies (CBDCs).

Additionally, one of the most significant challenges has been maintaining momentum. Activist fatigue is a real issue, especially when the opposition's resources seem inexhaustible. Prolonged campaigns can drain financial and human resources, leading to burnout among key figures in the movement. It's crucial for these groups to find sustainable ways to keep their efforts alive, both in terms of funding and volunteer engagement.

Interestingly, the formation of international coalitions has emerged as a double-edged sword. While these coalitions can combine resources and amplify their voices, they also face difficulties in coordinating strategies across different legal and cultural landscapes. Diverse political climates and agendas often lead to disagreements on the best approaches, causing friction and delays in action.

Youth engagement has proven to be one more area of both promise and peril. Younger generations are increasingly aware and concerned about issues of privacy and freedom, making them strong allies in resistance movements. However, their inherent skepticism towards traditional political structures can also result in fragmented efforts, as many prefer decentralized, grassroots approaches over organized political lobbying.

On a more optimistic note, the power of personal stories has proven effective in swaying public opinion. Testimonies from individuals affected by policies like digital ID and centralized economic controls have humanized these issues, making the abstract threats feel more tangible. Media interviews and viral social media posts have helped put faces to the resistance, thereby fostering empathy and support.

Another inspiring success is the emergence of new technologies that protect against invasive policies. Innovations in encrypted communications and decentralized currencies offer practical solutions to avoid the reach of government surveillance and financial control.

These technological advancements provide a glimmer of hope, showing that innovation can run counter to restrictive agendas.

However, critical to long-term success will be the cultivation of bipartisan support. Resistance movements have largely thrived on the fringes of established political spectrums, making it essential to find common ground with moderate entities. Adopting a more inclusive rhetoric that appeals to varied demographics can bolster the movement's legitimacy and reach.

In the end, the fight against the 2030 Agenda will not be swiftly concluded. It requires a coalition of the informed, the technologically savvy, and the passionate to continue pushing back against initiatives that threaten personal freedoms and economic independence. Only through sustained effort and strategic adaptations can resistance movements hope to achieve lasting success. The challenges are significant, but they are not insurmountable.

Chapter 21:
Legal Battles and Constitutional Rights

The clash between legal frameworks and the 2030 Agenda has ignited numerous court cases around the globe. Citizen groups, along with a handful of renegade politicians, have mounted significant legal challenges, questioning the constitutionality of certain agenda policies. One can't ignore the tension surrounding these court battles. They are, after all, a reflection of society's fear over loss of autonomy and personal freedoms.

Recent court cases shine a light on the growing unease. In the United States, there have been several landmark cases questioning the government's expansive surveillance measures, citing violations of the Fourth Amendment. Judges have been divided, with some ruling in favor of maintaining citizen privacy and others asserting that such measures are necessary for national security. The dichotomy within the judiciary mirrors the broader societal debate.

On the other side of the Atlantic, European courts are facing their own unique set of challenges. In countries such as Germany and France, issues related to digital identity have taken center stage. GDPR, celebrated for its stringent data protection laws, often comes into conflict with the broader surveillance measures proposed under the 2030 Agenda. This legal tug-of-war reveals the friction between collective goals and individual rights.

Moreover, these legal battles aren't just confined to privacy concerns. Financial freedoms are another hotly contested domain.

Central Bank Digital Currencies (CBDCs) are frequently under scrutiny. Critics argue that CBDCs can potentially lead to unprecedented government control over personal finances. Court cases in several nations have emerged, questioning the legality of such control mechanisms and advocating for greater financial privacy rights.

Throughout these cases, a recurring theme arises: the question of what constitutes an overreach of governmental power. The concept of "rights under threat" isn't just a legal issue but a fundamental societal concern. Whether it's about personal data, financial autonomy, or even the right to dissent, these legal battles encapsulate the essence of democratic resistance.

It's evident that the judiciary will play a critical role in defining the future trajectory of the 2030 Agenda. As citizens become more aware, and as advocacy groups become more organized, these legal skirmishes are likely to intensify. The courts, acting as the last bastion of individual rights, bear the heavy responsibility of balancing progress with preservation of freedom. In the end, the outcomes of these battles will shape how nations approach governance in an increasingly interconnected world.

Recent Court Cases

Legal battles surrounding the 2030 Agenda have been making headlines in courts across the globe. These cases are essential because they show how the agenda is being challenged and resisted through legal channels. They highlight conflicts between proponents of global governance and defenders of national sovereignty and individual freedoms. Some of these legal battles set precedents that have far-reaching implications for the future of personal and economic liberty.

In the United States, several cases have emerged that challenge various aspects of the 2030 Agenda. One notable case involved a dispute over land rights in rural areas. Farmers and landowners banded together to challenge regulations that they argued were designed to curtail their property rights in favor of central planning and environmental mandates. The plaintiffs claimed these regulations interfered with their ability to use their land as they saw fit, essentially arguing that they were being forced to comply with an international agenda that had no legal standing in the U.S. Constitution. The courts were faced with a difficult balance: protecting individual property rights while also considering broader environmental goals. The outcome of this case was critical in determining how far local jurisdictions could go in enforcing international guidelines.

Another significant case involved a state's decision to incorporate parts of the 2030 Agenda into its public education system. Parents filed lawsuits arguing that the curriculum changes were a form of indoctrination, designed to promote a particular globalist ideology rather than educate. They contended that this violated their rights to direct the upbringing and education of their children. This case gained traction and was eventually heard at the federal level, attracting widespread media attention. The final ruling upheld the parents' concerns to some extent, demanding a review of the controversial educational materials.

Across the Atlantic, European courts have also been busy. In the United Kingdom, a group of privacy advocates challenged the government's implementation of a Digital ID program, which they claimed was a direct infringement on individual privacy rights. The plaintiffs argued that such measures would lay the groundwork for a surveillance state, fundamentally altering the relationship between citizens and the state. The court ruled on the side of the privacy advocates, ordering a temporary halt to the program pending further review. This ruling sent shockwaves through the corridors of power, as it was a direct challenge to one of the 2030 Agenda's critical components.

Meanwhile, in Canada, several provincial governments have enacted laws that critics say align too closely with the 2030 Agenda, especially regarding environmental regulations and digital tracking. Business owners, particularly those in the energy sector, have initiated court cases claiming that these laws overstep constitutional boundaries. They argue that such regulations impose unnecessary burdens that stifle economic freedom and innovation. One landmark case saw an energy company suing the provincial government for damages, claiming that stringent environmental rules had effectively forced them out of business. The court's decision in favor of the company marked a significant victory for opponents of the 2030 Agenda.

Australia is another battleground, where legal challenges have been particularly fierce regarding government control over financial systems. One recent case involved a coalition of small business owners who argued that new financial regulations inspired by the 2030 Agenda were excessively restrictive. These regulations, according to the plaintiffs, made it almost impossible for them to access traditional banking services, thereby stifacing their ability to operate. The court's decision to strike down key parts of these regulations was hailed as a victory for economic freedom, setting an important legal precedent.

In Asia, the situation has been different but no less contentious. In India, the introduction of a social credit system prompted a furious backlash. Civil rights organizations quickly mobilized, arguing that such a system would severely restrict individual freedoms and create a society of surveillance and control. Several court challenges ensued, with the plaintiffs arguing that the social credit system violated the country's constitutional protections on privacy and freedom of movement. In a landmark ruling, the Indian Supreme Court agreed, effectively halting the implementation of the social credit system and dealing a significant blow to the proponents of the 2030 Agenda.

Legal battles also extend to the realm of digital privacy worldwide. Recently, a consortium of tech companies and digital rights advocates filed lawsuits against governments implementing aggressive data harvesting practices. These lawsuits argue that such practices are not only invasive but also unnecessary under the guise of improving public safety and efficiency. Courts in various jurisdictions have responded differently, but there has been a noticeable trend toward recognizing the importance of safeguarding individual privacy against overreach.

Each of these legal battles underscores a fundamental tension: the push for a globally coordinated approach to governance versus the preservation of local autonomy and individual rights. These court cases are crucial because they do more than resolve individual disputes; they set legal precedents that will shape future policies and potentially slow down or even halt the implementation of the 2030 Agenda's most controversial aspects.

It's important to note that the outcomes of these cases are by no means uniform. Some courts have ruled in favor of the agenda, citing broader benefits and the necessity of collective action in addressing global challenges. Others have sided with opponents, emphasizing the importance of constitutional protections and individual freedoms. This mixed bag of rulings creates a complex legal landscape, one that is constantly evolving and worth close attention.

What becomes clear from these recent court cases is that the 2030 Agenda is igniting powerful legal and civic debates. The courts are becoming a crucial arena where the battles over individual versus collective rights are being fought. These cases will have long-lasting implications, not only for the legal frameworks within countries but also for the very concept of governance in the 21st century.

Rights Under Threat

As we delve into the intricate web of legal battles and constitutional rights, it becomes apparent that the 2030 Agenda isn't just a set of lofty goals but a harbinger of sweeping changes. Central to this discussion are the rights under threat—those liberties that have long been the bedrock of democratic societies but now stand on precarious ground.

Imagine a world where the government knows your every move, every transaction, and every conversation. This isn't a dystopian fantasy but a potential future under the encroaching reach of policies tied to the 2030 Agenda. From Digital IDs to Central Bank Digital Currencies (CBDCs), the mechanisms set to be implemented can track and control facets of our lives in ways we couldn't have fathomed just a decade ago.

Consider the principle of financial privacy. With the advent of CBDCs, traditional cash transactions—those anonymous exchanges that offer a semblance of privacy—could become obsolete. Governments would have unprecedented access to your spending habits, investments, and even philanthropic contributions. The implications stretch beyond mere oversight; they extend into social control. A government disapproving of your expenditures could freeze accounts or limit your access to services.

The erosion of privacy does not stop with finances. The increasing push for Digital IDs, purportedly to streamline services and combat fraud, carries significant risks. These digital identifiers could become a requisite for accessing basic services and amenities—a mechanism that links your every action to a centralized database. Such a system, while efficient, is ripe for abuse. Data breaches, identity theft, or even misuse by governmental bodies are genuine concerns.

Legal precedents show a mixed bag of upholding and eroding constitutional rights. Recent court cases reveal an alarming tendency toward prioritizing state security and surveillance over individual freedoms. The balance has shifted subtly, often under the guise of national security or public health. For instance, mandatory data sharing between tech companies and governments, once a controversial idea, has gained traction. Such policies don't just infringe upon the right to privacy but set a dangerous precedent.

The right to free speech is another casualty in this evolving scenario. Increasingly, we see tighter controls over what can be expressed online. Social media platforms, wielding significant influence, are pressured to censor content that doesn't align with official narratives. Governments have not hesitated to implement laws that penalize what they term as "misinformation." This isn't just a clampdown on falsehoods; it's a broad umbrella that often stifles dissent and critical thinking.

But the specter of control doesn't end online. In many regions, peaceful protests are met with severe crackdowns. Under the pretext of maintaining order, assemblies are disbanded, and activists are arrested. Laws that once protected peaceful assembly and protest are being reinterpreted or outright rewritten to fit the new narrative of security and control.

Alarmingly, these legal shifts are not occurring in isolation. International coalitions and global governance models, as promoted by entities like the United Nations and the World Economic Forum, push these agendas further under the justification of a unified effort against global challenges. While the idea of global cooperation is inherently positive, it becomes perilous when it overrides national sovereignty and individual rights.

The right to property also hangs in the balance. The rhetoric of "You will own nothing, and be happy," though often dismissed as hyperbole, underscores a real threat to personal ownership. Policies aided by the 2030 Agenda advocate for communal ownership models and rental economies, subtly eroding the sanctity of personal property. The implications for small businesses and entrepreneurs are dire—

without ownership, economic freedom diminishes, leading to a dependent populace.

In this landscape, who safeguards our rights? Judicial systems, historically the bastions of constitutional rights, are under immense pressure. Courtrooms are becoming battlegrounds where the line between safeguarding freedoms and promoting societal safety blurs. Jurisdictions around the world grapple with cases that will set precedents for years to come. And though some victories uphold individual liberties, there is an unsettling trend toward favoring state control.

A central figure in navigating these tumultuous waters is the informed citizenry. Awareness and activism form the bedrock of resistance against the encroachments of the 2030 Agenda. Knowledge of one's rights and the potential threats is crucial. Advocacy groups, legal experts, and civil liberties organizations are increasingly vocal, urging judicial and legislative bodies to tread carefully.

Grassroots movements and local interventions highlight resistance. From court battles over surveillance laws to advocacy for financial privacy, the fight spans multiple fronts. Even in the face of sweeping global agendas, local victories provide a beacon of hope. They remind us that while rights are under threat, they are not yet lost.

As we advance, the responsibility to preserve and protect these rights doesn't solely rest with lawmakers or judges. It demands vigilance and action from every individual. The narrative of rights under threat isn't merely an academic discussion; it is a clarion call to recognize, resist, and reclaim the spaces of freedom that form the core of our societies.

Chapter 22:
International Coalitions Against
the 2030 Agenda

In recent years, the 2030 Agenda has faced rising opposition from a spectrum of international coalitions. These groups, often consisting of countries, NGOs, and independent organizations, have banded together to push back against what they perceive as overreaching global governance.

One of the most notable of these alliances is the Sovereignty Coalition, an assembly of nations determined to maintain their economic and political autonomy. This coalition argues that the 2030 Agenda's policies undermine national sovereignty and impose uniform regulations that do not account for regional differences. Their collective message is clear: one-size-fits-all solutions do not work for a world as diverse as ours.

The Liberty Network, a consortium of libertarian think tanks and advocacy organizations, also stands out in the fight against the 2030 Agenda. They focus on promoting individual freedoms and limited government intervention, viewing the Agenda's initiatives as a direct threat to these principles.

In Europe, the Freedom League is a notable player. Comprised of several member countries and grassroots movements, this coalition emphasizes transparency and democratic participation, arguing that the 2030 Agenda has been pushed with little public consultation.

Through campaigns and legal challenges, they strive to ensure that citizens have a say in policies that impact their lives.

Despite differing motivations, these coalitions share a common goal: to protect personal freedoms and national independence against an increasingly centralized global plan. Their methods include lobbying, public awareness campaigns, and legal actions designed to expose the Agenda's more controversial aspects.

Efforts to preserve freedoms have not been limited to reactive measures alone. Proactive initiatives are also gaining traction, particularly those aimed at promoting alternative development models. These initiatives seek to foster sustainable growth while respecting national boundaries and individual liberties.

For these coalitions, the fight against the 2030 Agenda is as much a battle of ideology as it is of policy. They believe that preserving the very essence of a democratic and free society is at stake. While their paths may differ, their rallying cry remains unified: resist global homogenization, and champion liberty and sovereignty.

Prominent Global Alliances

In the labyrinthine web of international politics, numerous prominent global alliances have emerged, with the singular aim of countering the sweeping implications of the 2030 Agenda. These alliances consist of an eclectic mix of nations, organizations, and grassroots movements. Despite diverse political, economic, and cultural backgrounds, these entities share a common goal: to uphold national sovereignty and individual freedoms threatened by the agenda.

A significant player in this arena is the Visegrád Group, comprising Hungary, Poland, the Czech Republic, and Slovakia. These Central European countries have consistently voiced their opposition to the centralized global governance advocated by the 2030 Agenda. For them, the agenda represents a bureaucratic overreach that threatens national autonomy. Their strategy involves tightening border controls, rejecting multinational regulations, and implementing policies that prioritize national interests over global agendas.

Another vital coalition is the Quadrilateral Security Dialogue, involving the United States, India, Japan, and Australia. Although initially formed to counterbalance China's rising influence in the Indo-Pacific region, this alliance has increasingly focused on broader issues of global governance and economic sovereignty. The Quad's strategy revolves around bolstering cybersecurity, ensuring free and fair trade, and maintaining open maritime routes—an integrated approach to counter any overreach implied by the 2030 Agenda.

In Latin America, the Lima Group, initially established to address the crisis in Venezuela, has broadened its scope to counteract elements of the 2030 Agenda they perceive as infringing on national sovereignty. Comprising over a dozen countries, including Argentina, Brazil, and Canada, the Lima Group emphasizes diplomatic engagement and regional solidarity to challenge any external influences that undermine their independence.

Europe also sees resistant coalitions forming. Notably, the "Three Seas Initiative," which includes 12 European Union member states, aims to foster economic and infrastructural development independently of central EU policies aligned with the 2030 Agenda. By investing in regional projects, the initiative aims to maintain control over strategic assets and resource flows, thus preserving their autonomy from supranational dictates.

In Asia, ASEAN (Association of Southeast Asian Nations) members have created a united front to negotiate terms that favor national priorities over global commitments. Countries like Vietnam, Indonesia, and the Philippines are particularly vocal about the necessity of balancing international cooperation with preserving local governance structures. ASEAN's intricate diplomacy and shared regional objectives serve to resist external pressures to conform to global standards that do not fit their unique cultural and economic contexts.

Grassroots movements, too, have played a critical role in forming informal alliances that challenge the 2030 Agenda. For instance, agricultural unions in Europe, community organizations in Africa, and citizen assemblies in Latin America have coalesced to voice their collective opposition to global policies that threaten local industries and traditional ways of life. Though less formalized, these groups work tirelessly through protests, advocacy, and local governance to protect their rights and freedoms.

In North America, coalitions of states within the United States have taken legislative steps to counter the 2030 Agenda's perceived threats. States like Texas and Florida have introduced laws aimed at limiting federal overreach, emphasizing local governance, and protecting individual freedoms. These state-level actions often include safeguarding energy independence, refusing to implement digital ID systems, and blocking participation in international surveillance networks.

At a broader level, international NGOs and think tanks have become critical in forming alliances against the 2030 Agenda. Organizations like the Cato Institute, the Heritage Foundation, and the Atlas Network produce research and mobilize public opinion to challenge the sweeping reforms proposed under the agenda. Their work often highlights the risks to economic freedom, individual privacy, and democratic governance that could ensue if the agenda is fully implemented.

Moreover, various advocacy groups for digital rights, such as the Electronic Frontier Foundation and Privacy International, have joined forces to resist the digital surveillance and data collection elements championed by the 2030 Agenda. By promoting robust legal frameworks and fostering public awareness, these organizations aim to ensure that technological advancements do not come at the expense of civil liberties.

Internationally, there are also religious and ethical organizations that rally against aspects of the 2030 Agenda that they view as contrary to their moral values. For example, groups representing various religious denominations have expressed concern over specific agenda items and policies they interpret as undermining family structures and traditional moral frameworks. These groups often engage in lobbying, public campaigns, and direct dialogue with policymakers to advocate for their positions.

Despite being a patchwork of entities differing in scope, focus, and methodology, these alliances signify a growing global resistance dedicated to preserving national sovereignty and individual freedoms. As these coalitions gain momentum, their influence is felt not just in diplomatic corridors but also in the political discourse within each country, making it increasingly difficult for the 2030 Agenda to advance unchallenged.

In the light of these developments, it becomes clear that the opposition to the 2030 Agenda is not isolated or fragmented. Instead, it encompasses a broad coalition of states, regions, and civil society actors united by a common cause—resisting a global governance model they perceive as detrimental to sovereignty, freedom, and individual rights.

Efforts to Preserve Freedoms

As the global push for the 2030 Agenda intensifies, there's a growing counterforce made up of diverse international coalitions, united in their determination to safeguard individual liberties. These coalitions are not mere reactionary bodies; they represent a coordinated effort across multiple fronts, aiming to resist a future in which freedoms are systematically eroded. The 2030 Agenda, with its encompassing reach, has sparked significant concern among these groups, prompting them to take a stand.

Firstly, grassroots movements from various countries have banded together to form international alliances. These groups, often initiated by concerned citizens, focus on educating the public about the possible ramifications of globally mandated policies. They use online platforms, public gatherings, and informational campaigns to spread their message, emphasizing real-world examples of rights violations that could act as harbingers of the broader future. Through these efforts, they aim to raise awareness and rally more people to their cause.

In Europe, a notable coalition exists comprising organizations from countries like Hungary, Poland, and the Czech Republic. These entities highlight how the 2030 Agenda could undermine national sovereignty and impose a one-size-fits-all set of regulations that doesn't account for cultural and socio-economic differences. They propose alternative models that emphasize localized decision-making and respect for national particularities, arguing these would better serve the interests of their citizens.

Moving west, North American coalitions have gained traction, particularly in the United States and Canada. These groups often include a mix of political activists, academics, and ordinary citizens concerned about the potential for increased government overreach. They frequently collaborate with think tanks and policy institutes to draft white papers and policy proposals that criticize the 2030 Agenda. Moreover, these organizations call for the preservation of constitutional rights, fearing that international mandates could infringe upon freedoms guaranteed by national laws.

One such coalition based in the U.S., for example, has been relentless in its campaign to highlight the risks posed by central bank digital currencies (CBDCs). They use a variety of platforms to discuss how CBDCs could grant governments unprecedented control over financial transactions, effectively eliminating financial privacy. Their educational initiatives include webinars, podcasts, and articles that dissect the potential dangers of this technology and encourage public discourse on the issue. By increasing public awareness, these organizations aim to foster a climate of skepticism and critical evaluation regarding CBDCs.

On another front, several prominent international NGOs have turned their focus toward preserving digital privacy, recognizing the inherent risks in the increasing digitization of personal data. These organizations shed light on how surveillance technologies are being implemented under the guise of security and efficiency. Reports and case studies are frequently published detailing the potential misuse of such technologies, and how they could be weaponized to suppress dissent and control populations.

Moreover, legal defense funds have been set up to challenge violations of personal freedoms. Lawyers and human rights advocates volunteer their time to defend individuals who have been targeted due to surveillance, censorship, or coercion linked to the 2030 Agenda's aims. These legal battles are crucial, not only for the individuals involved but also for setting precedents that protect broader societal freedoms. Court victories in these areas serve as critical bulwarks against the encroachment of global mandates into the private sphere.

Besides these grassroots and legal efforts, there's also the sphere of academic and intellectual resistance. Scholars from a variety of disciplines—economics, political science, sociology—are questioning the underlying assumptions and empirical validity of the 2030 Agenda. In journals, books, and public lectures, these academics analyze and critique the Agenda from multiple angles, exposing its potential flaws and biases. This intellectual opposition provides a robust foundation for broader societal resistance, reinforcing the efforts of more practical, on-the-ground coalitions.

Social media has also emerged as a battleground for these coalitions. Activists use online platforms to circumvent traditional media channels, which often underreport or misrepresent their views. Through coordinated campaigns, they create viral content that resonates with a wide audience, transcending geographic and cultural boundaries. Hashtags, viral videos, and online petitions are among the tools employed to galvanize public opinion and build a transnational community of individuals committed to defending their freedoms.

It's also important to mention the role of independent journalists and alternative media outlets. These entities take on the crucial task of investigating and reporting on the actions and implications of the 2030 Agenda, often at great personal and professional risk. They offer a narrative that counters the mainstream portrayal, providing a platform for voices that warning about the potential loss of freedoms.

Lastly, some coalitions seek to influence policy directly through lobbying efforts. They engage with sympathetic politicians and policymakers, advocating for legislative measures that counteract the more draconian aspects of the 2030 Agenda. This form of activism ensures that there is a constant political pressure against the enactment of laws that could diminish personal and national sovereignties.

In summary, the efforts to preserve freedoms in the face of the 2030 Agenda are multifaceted and deeply interconnected. From grassroots activism and academic critique to legal defenses and political lobbying, various international coalitions are working tirelessly to ensure that individual liberties are not sacrificed on the altar of global conformity. It is a complex, ongoing battle, but one that gathers momentum and strength with every passing day.

Chapter 23:
Media and Public Perception

The 2030 Agenda is not just about plans and policies; it is about how these plans are communicated to the public. Media plays an instrumental role in shaping public perception, often acting as the bridge between the policymakers and the populace. The way this agenda is portrayed in the media can significantly influence how it is received and, consequently, how individuals and communities react to it.

Media narratives are powerful. A single news story can change opinions overnight, stoking fear or fostering acceptance. Phrases like "The Great Reset" have gained different interpretations depending on who's delivering the news. Some media outlets present it as a positive shift towards a more equitable world, while others warn of impending doom and loss of freedoms. This dichotomy in reporting creates a divided public, where opinions are shaped not by facts, but by the lens through which these facts are shown.

How the 2030 Agenda is framed matters. Headlines that highlight sustainability and global cooperation can make the agenda seem like a noble cause, even if there are underlying issues. Conversely, focusing on potential overreach and monitoring can fuel skepticism and resistance. Both sides usually rely on selective reporting, emphasizing what aligns with their intended narrative and sidelining or downplaying what doesn't.

Shaping public opinion isn't just about news articles and television segments. Social media has become an influential platform where narratives are not just shared, but also dissected and debated. Memes, hashtags, and viral videos can effectively create echo chambers, reinforcing existing beliefs and making it hard for alternative viewpoints to break through. In such spaces, the 2030 Agenda can be both a beacon of hope and a harbinger of tyranny, depending on whose feed you're following.

The role of journalists and content creators is crucial. In an ideal world, they would provide balanced and nuanced views on the 2030 Agenda, allowing the public to form educated opinions. However, media is a business, and sensationalism often sells better than balanced reporting. This commercialization of content means that the public might never get the full picture, leading to a skewed perception of what the 2030 Agenda actually entails.

Ultimately, understanding the media's influence on public perception is key to deciphering the prevailing sentiments about the 2030 Agenda. How we consume media and who controls the narratives will continue to play pivotal roles in either clarifying or complicating our understanding of future policies and their impacts on our lives.

Influence of Media Narratives

The media holds immense power. By shaping narratives, it can influence public perception in ways that few other institutions can match. When it comes to the 2030 Agenda, the media's role cannot be understated. How reporters frame issues, the headlines that make it to our screens, and the voices that get amplified all shape how we think and feel about this complex global initiative.

Media narratives can often create a sense of urgency or apathy, depending on how they frame the Agenda. For instance, headlines that emphasize imminent danger or catastrophic outcomes can lead to heightened public anxiety. In contrast, articles that focus on potential benefits and successful implementations might lull the public into a false sense of security, making them less scrutinizing and more accepting of the Agenda's more controversial elements.

The choice of language in media reports plays a critical role too. Terms like "sustainability" and "global cooperation" may evoke positive connotations, whereas words such as "control" and "surveillance" stir distrust and fear. Thus, a biased choice of terminology can steer public discourse in a particular direction. When the media repeatedly uses euphemisms and positive jargon, it can downplay the more alarming aspects of the 2030 Agenda.

Another layer to consider is the medium through which information is disseminated. Traditional news outlets like newspapers and television still wield significant influence but social media platforms are arguably more impactful in today's digital age. The viral nature of social media allows narratives to spread swiftly, often without thorough fact-checking. In such a landscape, misinformation and selective storytelling can easily become intertwined with genuine news, further distorting public perception.

It's crucial to understand that the media isn't a monolith; it comprises various entities with different motivations and biases. Some publications might staunchly support the 2030 Agenda, citing its potential to address climate change and socio-economic inequalities. Others may focus on the potential pitfalls, such as the erosion of personal freedoms and economic sovereignty. Unfortunately, this polarization often leads to echo chambers where audiences only consume content that aligns with their preconceived beliefs, exacerbating division and misunderstanding.

Public perception is also heavily influenced by the credibility of the sources cited in media narratives. Expert opinions and official statements can lend weight to a story. However, the selection of these authorities is telling. When media platforms predominantly feature experts who support the 2030 Agenda, dissenting voices are marginalized, creating an illusion of unanimous approval. Conversely, giving a platform exclusively to critics paints a picture of widespread opposition and skepticism.

The timing and prominence of news stories are other critical factors. Major events or new data related to the 2030 Agenda often receive prime coverage, stirring public debate. Yet, the decision about what constitutes "newsworthy" information can reflect underlying agendas. Smaller, local impacts may be underreported compared to grandiose, global milestones, skewing public perception toward the latter.

The potential for media narratives to act as a form of soft power cannot be ignored. Governments and organizations frequently engage in public relations campaigns to sway public opinion. Sponsorships, advertisements, and editorial influences can subtly yet effectively mold narratives to align with particular interests. For example, philanthropic donations by influential individuals to media outlets can sometimes buy favorable coverage, shaping the narrative in a way that aligns with their objectives.

Real-world consequences often arise from media-driven perceptions. Public opinion, shaped by media narratives, can influence policy decisions and political outcomes. Lawmakers are keenly aware of the electorate's views, and a media landscape saturated with particular interpretations of the 2030 Agenda can lead to significant policy shifts. For instance, heightened public concerns about digital surveillance could compel politicians to enact stricter privacy regulations, while overwhelming support for sustainability initiatives might accelerate green policy adoption.

Furthermore, the role of media extends beyond simply reporting events. Investigative journalism can expose hidden aspects of the 2030 Agenda, uncovering stories that the public might otherwise never learn about. This form of deep-dive reporting can reveal conflicts of interest, financial backers, and unintended consequences, adding layers of complexity to the narrative that simple headlines can't capture.

Educational content, documentaries, and in-depth analysis programs further contribute to shaping perceptions. These formats allow for more nuanced discussions, providing a full spectrum of viewpoints. However, the accessibility and popularity of these forms of media vary, meaning that not all audiences are equally informed.

Given these multifaceted influences, consumers of media must cultivate a critical approach. Evaluating sources, cross-referencing information, and being wary of sensationalism are essential steps toward a more balanced understanding of the 2030 Agenda. Mindful media consumption can mitigate some of the biases and manipulations inherent in current narratives.

In conclusion, the influence of media narratives on public perception of the 2030 Agenda is profound and far-reaching. By understanding the mechanics of media influence, individuals are better equipped to navigate the flood of information they encounter daily. The stakes are high, as these perceptions ultimately shape the societal and political landscape we collectively inhabit. Through informed consumption of media, we can strive for a more balanced, less manipulated view, critical for preserving personal freedoms and genuine democratic discourse.

Shaping Public Opinion

The media's role in shaping public opinion about the 2030 Agenda cannot be overstated. From the headlines we read to the social media posts we scroll through, narratives are being crafted, dissected, and then reassembled to deliver messages that influence our perception. Most people are aware that media channels can sway public sentiment, but the extent and methods by which they do so are often overlooked.

At the heart of this influence is agenda-setting, a concept closely linked to the media's power. Agenda-setting works by making certain issues seem more important than others. When a particular topic like the 2030 Agenda is repeatedly highlighted in news reports, talk shows, and online discussions, it occupies a dominant position in the public's mind. People start to view this issue as crucial, regardless of its real-world significancecompared to other matters. This issue-placement isn't random but a carefully crafted plan aimed at steering public discourse in a specific direction.

Media outlets are not uniform; they differ in ownership, editorial policies, and political leanings. Mainstream media companies often have vested interests that align with political or corporate power structures. Their coverage, whether it's print, digital, or broadcast, tends to reflect the interests and perspectives of these powerful entities. The 2030 Agenda might be presented either as a utopian vision for a sustainable future or as a dystopian nightmare of government control, depending on the outlet's bias.

Another critical facet is framing. Framing goes beyond highlighting certain issues; it involves presenting those issues in specific ways that evoke particular reactions. For example, terms like "green economy" and "sustainable development" can evoke positive reactions and a sense of urgency. On the other hand, words like "regulations", "restrictions", and "government overreach" can provoke fear and resistance. The choice of words in media coverage plays a significant role in shaping opinions about the 2030 Agenda. These word choices can influence not just what people think about but how they think about it.

Language, visuals, and even the selection of experts and analysts play crucial roles in framing. When an expert speaks on a topic, their credentials and affiliations usually lend authority to their views. But who gets to be called an "expert"? Often, it's those whose opinions align with the media outlet's slant. By selectively featuring certain experts over others, media platforms can reinforce their desired narrative about the 2030 Agenda, subtly steering public perception.

Social media has added a complex layer to this landscape. Unlike traditional media, social media platforms are not bound by journalistic standards, and anyone can post their opinion, creating a cacophony of voices. Algorithms prioritize content that gains more engagement, which often means sensationalistic, emotional, or controversial takes rise to the top. This can create echo chambers where individuals are exposed predominantly to views that confirm their pre-existing beliefs, exacerbating polarization. The 2030 Agenda can thus become a lightning rod for misinformation, conspiracy theories, or outright propaganda, depending on the contours of one's social media bubble.

Moreover, the phenomenon of "fake news" complicates the matter. Disinformation campaigns can be launched to either discredit the 2030 Agenda or falsely promote it. Whether it's manipulated statistics, out-of-context quotes, or completely fabricated stories, such tactics aim to distort reality. The sheer volume and velocity of information make it challenging for the average person to discern fact from fiction, leaving public opinion vulnerable to manipulation.

Advertising and sponsored content are other subtle yet powerful tools. Even when people believe they are consuming unbiased information, they are often subject to cleverly disguised advertisements or sponsored news articles. These paid pieces often carry specific agendas, and readers may not always recognize them as such. Campaigns promoting the supposed benefits or highlighting the alleged dangers of the 2030 Agenda can thus blend seamlessly into the broader media narrative, shaping opinions at a subconscious level.

A media landscape characterized by a high level of consolidation further exacerbates these issues. When a handful of conglomerates own the majority of media outlets, the diversity of viewpoints shrinks. These conglomerates can produce and distribute content that follows a homogeneous, consolidated narrative. When it comes to the 2030 Agenda, this can mean a unified message being drummed into the public mind, leaving little room for dissent or alternative perspectives.

Ultimately, shaping public opinion about the 2030 Agenda involves a sophisticated interplay of agenda-setting, framing, selective expert consultation, social media dynamics, disinformation, advertising, and media consolidation. These elements interact in a complex web that does more than inform—it shapes how people think and feel about this global initiative. Awareness of these mechanisms is the first step towards critically engaging with the information presented to us, encouraging a more nuanced and informed public discourse.

Understanding these dynamics is crucial not just for consumers of information but also for activists, policymakers, and anyone engaged in the broader dialogue about the 2030 Agenda. Being aware of how public opinion is shaped can lead to more effective communication strategies and, ultimately, actions that align more closely with democratic principles and individual freedoms. Without this awareness, we risk becoming passive recipients of orchestrated narratives, rather than active participants in the democratic process.

Chapter 24:
Future Projections and Scenarios

The 2030 Agenda has sparked considerable debate, with its ambitious goals and sweeping changes. As we look toward the future, several possible outcomes emerge, each with its own set of implications for personal freedom, governmental power, and societal structure. It is essential to understand these scenarios to prepare effectively for the coming years.

One possible projection is the complete realization of the 2030 Agenda as envisioned by its architects. In this scenario, governments may have unprecedented control over financial systems, personal data, and individual freedoms. Central Bank Digital Currencies (CBDCs) could become the norm, potentially eroding financial privacy and autonomy. Digital IDs might be mandatory, making it nearly impossible to participate in society without constant surveillance. If these elements align, there could be a significant reduction in personal ownership and control over personal assets.

Alternatively, we could see a fragmented implementation of the Agenda, with different regions and countries adopting parts of it to varying degrees. This uneven application could create a patchwork of policies and standards, resulting in a chaotic global landscape. In some areas, personal freedoms might be preserved, while in others, government control could tighten. The disparity might lead to cross-border tensions and conflicts, as people and capital move to regions with more favorable conditions.

A more optimistic scenario involves strong resistance and pushback against the 2030 Agenda. In this case, grassroots movements, legal battles, and international coalitions could slow or halt the implementation of the most controversial elements. Advocacy for personal freedom and economic independence might gain traction, curbing the reach of digital surveillance and government control. This scenario requires robust civil engagement and a concerted effort to uphold individual rights.

Technological advancements will also play a critical role in shaping the future. Emerging technologies could either enhance surveillance capabilities or empower individuals to protect their privacy and freedoms. Innovations in encryption, decentralized systems, and privacy-focused tools might provide counterbalances to centralization efforts. Keeping an eye on these technological trends is crucial for anyone concerned about the long-term impacts of the 2030 Agenda.

We must also consider the socio-economic implications of these scenarios. In a world where personal ownership becomes obsolete, the concept of work and compensation could drastically change. Universal Basic Income (UBI) might become a standard policy to address unemployment caused by automation. However, the societal impact of a widespread UBI system remains unpredictable. Will it foster a culture of innovation and creativity, or will it lead to complacency and dependence?

Environmental considerations can't be overlooked either. The 2030 Agenda places a strong emphasis on sustainability and climate action. While these goals are commendable, their implementation could bring about significant economic and social shifts. The transition to green energy and sustainable practices might disrupt industries, leading to job losses and economic upheaval in the short term. However, it also offers opportunities for new industries and economic models to emerge.

In conclusion, the future under the 2030 Agenda is uncertain and full of potential pitfalls and opportunities. Various scenarios present different challenges and highlight the importance of staying informed and engaged. Preparing for the future means not only understanding these projections but also actively participating in the conversation to shape the world we want to live in. The journey ahead is complex, but awareness and action can make a significant difference.

Possible Outcomes

As we delve into the future projections and scenarios surrounding the 2030 Agenda, it's essential to examine the potential outcomes that might arise from its implementation. Considering the broad scope of this agenda and the sweeping changes it envisions, the range of possible outcomes is vast and varied.

One conceivable outcome is a world where individual ownership is severely curtailed. The idea that "you will own nothing and be happy," as promoted by the proponents of the Great Reset, could manifest in various forms. People might lease or share everything, from homes to vehicles, diminishing personal assets and altering the very fabric of economic independence. Such a shift could undermine personal autonomy and lead to increased dependency on centralized entities for basic necessities.

Another outcome involves significant governmental control over financial systems. With the adoption of Central Bank Digital Currencies (CBDCs), governments could gain unprecedented oversight and regulation capabilities. This scenario could enable real-time tracking of financial transactions, thereby facilitating tighter control over citizens' spending behaviors. While proponents argue this could enhance security and streamline economic policies, critics fear it might pave the way for intrusive surveillance and limitations on financial freedom.

In the realm of personal freedom and privacy, the implementation of digital IDs could create a comprehensive and intrusive monitoring system. This project could collect vast amounts of personal data, from healthcare records to financial activities. Such a system might be marketed as enhancing efficiency and safety, but it could also be exploited for mass surveillance, eroding privacy rights and personal liberties.

Social credit systems, akin to the one currently operational in China, could emerge on a global scale. These systems, which rank and score citizens based on various behaviors, could profoundly impact daily life. Travel restrictions, access to services, and even employment opportunities could become contingent on maintaining a favorable social score. The implications for social cohesion and individual freedoms are profound and troubling, raising the specter of a highly monitored and controlled society.

The potential for economic repercussions on small businesses and entrepreneurs is another significant concern. The sweeping changes proposed by the 2030 Agenda might favor large corporations and governments, sidelining smaller enterprises. This could stifle innovation, limit economic mobility, and concentrate economic power in the hands of a few. Jobs and livelihoods could be lost, leading to a widening gap between the economic elite and the general population.

Additionally, the educational landscape could be transformed by policies aimed at indoctrinating youth. Curricular changes designed to align with the 2030 Agenda's goals might shape the perspectives and beliefs of future generations. This could result in a homogenized worldview, emphasizing collective goals at the expense of individual critical thinking and intellectual freedom. The long-term implications for society and democratic values could be significant.

Strategically, nations might form international coalitions to either support or resist the Agenda. Countries that embrace its principles might work closely together, creating blocs that push for global governance and unified policies. Conversely, nations opposing the Agenda's stipulations might band together to preserve their sovereignty and protect individual freedoms. These alignments could reshape geopolitical landscapes, with alliances and conflicts potentially arising around these ideological lines.

The influence of Big Tech in this paradigm is substantial. Technology companies, with their vast data harvesting capabilities, could play a critical role in shaping and implementing the 2030 Agenda. Data privacy concerns are paramount, with these companies potentially using harvested data to influence public opinion, monitor behavior, and enforce compliance. The lines between corporate and governmental power might blur further, with significant implications for democracy and citizen autonomy.

In the media realm, narratives concerning the 2030 Agenda will be critical in shaping public perception. Media outlets that promote the Agenda's goals might frame it as a path to a sustainable and equitable future. On the other hand, voices of dissent might be marginalized or silenced, creating a one-sided portrayal that stifles critical debate and dissenting viewpoints. This shaping of public discourse could significantly impact democratic processes and the ability of citizens to make informed choices.

Resilience and resistance movements are likely to emerge in response to these sweeping changes. Activists and advocacy groups might seek to preserve personal freedoms and counteract what they see as overreach by global organizations and governments. The success of these movements will depend on their ability to mobilize, raise awareness, and influence policy. Legal battles and constitutional rights challenges could also play a pivotal role in resisting aspects of the Agenda that infringe on civil liberties and national sovereignty.

In summary, the range of possible outcomes stemming from the 2030 Agenda is broad and complex. While some envision a utopian future of shared prosperity and sustainability, others warn of dystopian scenarios marked by loss of personal freedoms, economic disparity, and intrusive surveillance. The actual trajectory will likely lie somewhere between these extremes, shaped by a myriad of factors, including political will, technological advances, and public response. As the Agenda unfolds, vigilance and critical analysis will be essential in navigating its implications and safeguarding fundamental rights and freedoms.

Preparing for the Future

The 2030 Agenda brings with it an array of concerns that can seem both overwhelming and intimidating. One of the most crucial steps in addressing these concerns is preparing for the future. This involves not only understanding the possible scenarios that could unfold but also equipping ourselves with the tools and resources necessary to navigate these turbulent waters. As we delve deeper into the intricacies of the 2030 Agenda, it's essential to adopt a proactive stance, one that anticipates changes and adapts accordingly.

The first step in preparation is education. Knowledge is power, and the more we understand about the 2030 Agenda, the better equipped we'll be to address its challenges. This doesn't just mean a superficial understanding; it requires a comprehensive grasp of the policies and initiatives being proposed. Educational resources, workshops, and seminars can play a pivotal role in this. Communities need to come together to share information and strategies that can be used to push back against potentially harmful policies.

Financial preparedness is another critical aspect. With the possibility of greater government control over financial systems, including the introduction of Central Bank Digital Currencies (CBDCs), it's essential to diversify personal assets. Investing in a mix of traditional assets such as precious metals, stocks, and even cryptocurrencies can serve as a hedge against potential disruptions. Creating emergency funds and reducing debts can also ensure financial stability in uncertain times.

Moreover, digital privacy measures can't be overlooked. As governments push toward digital IDs and surveillance, protecting personal data becomes paramount. Utilizing encryption tools, secure communication channels, and privacy-focused software can provide a layer of protection against unwarranted intrusions. Being vigilant about digital footprints and understanding the implications of data sharing are vital steps in safeguarding privacy.

Community-building is another crucial strategy. By fostering strong local networks, individuals can rely on each other for support and resources. Whether it's through forming local cooperatives, community gardens, or mutual aid networks, the strength of a community can serve as a buffer against external pressures. This local resilience can also provide a sense of solidarity and shared purpose, which is essential in facing large-scale changes.

Health and wellness shouldn't be sidelined either. Ensuring access to quality healthcare, emphasizing preventive measures, and maintaining physical and mental well-being are vital. A robust health system within a community can mitigate the impact of widespread changes and policies that might affect personal freedoms. Regular health check-ups, fitness routines, and mental health support can collectively fortify an individual's ability to withstand the stress associated with these uncertainties.

It's also important to engage in political activism. Understanding local, national, and international policies and their implications on personal freedoms can guide effective advocacy. Staying informed about legislation, participating in community meetings, and supporting leaders who prioritize individual liberties are actions that contribute to the larger fight. Grassroots organizations and movements that focus on these aspects can amplify individual efforts and provide larger platforms for dissent and dialogue.

Legal knowledge can be an asset in these times. Being aware of constitutional rights and the legal protections available can empower individuals to stand up against overreach. Legal literacy programs and consultations with legal experts can demystify complex legal jargon and make it accessible to the general public. Understanding the boundaries of lawful versus unlawful actions by the state can guide measured and informed responses.

Preparing for the future also involves ecological awareness. Sustainability practices such as community-based farming, permaculture, and resource conservation can reduce dependency on centralized systems. Localized food production not only ensures food security but also strengthens community ties. Embracing renewable energy sources and eco-friendly technologies can diminish reliance on traditional power grids, making communities more self-sufficient.

Adopting a flexible mindset is key. The ability to adapt to changing circumstances stems from a combination of preparedness and open-mindedness. Regularly reassessing plans and strategies in light of new information can prevent complacency. Flexibility also entails a willingness to learn and unlearn, to pivot strategies when necessary, and to embrace innovative solutions.

Building alliances with like-minded groups and individuals across borders can magnify efforts. International coalitions that resist the 2030 Agenda can provide support, share resources, and offer new perspectives. These alliances can create a united front that champions personal freedoms and autonomy on a global scale, reinforcing the notion that the fight for individual liberties transcends geographical boundaries.

Preparing for the future is not a solitary endeavor. It's a collective journey that requires awareness, action, and collaboration. By leveraging knowledge, fostering community spirit, and adopting a proactive stance, we can navigate the challenges posed by the 2030 Agenda. Ultimately, the goal is to preserve personal freedoms and ensure a future where individual rights are upheld and respected.

Chapter 25:
Building a Sustainable
Fight for Freedom

The path to maintaining freedom in the face of the 2030 Agenda is a marathon, not a sprint. There is an urgency that cannot be understated, but the fight for freedom and personal autonomy requires a comprehensive and sustainable approach. This chapter explores long-term strategies and ways to mobilize effectively for maximum impact.

First, understanding the nature of power and control is crucial. The 2030 Agenda is not a static document; it is a dynamic blueprint that adapts and evolves. Recognizing this flexibility means that our responses must also be adaptable. Static resistance often leads to quick suppression, but dynamic approaches can elicit more lasting change. Think of the fight for freedom as an ongoing dialogue rather than a final battle. It requires constant vigilance and adaptability.

Central to any sustainable movement is strong grassroots organization. Large-scale mobilizations often start at the local level. Begin by fostering awareness within your community. Local groups can serve as the backbone for broader resistance networks. Hosting town halls, workshops, and educational events can amplify knowledge and galvanize collective action. Grassroots efforts not only build a sense of community but also create a diversified foundation that is harder to dismantle.

Technology offers both a challenge and an opportunity. While digital tracking and surveillance are real threats, they can also be harnessed to fight back. Encrypted communication channels, decentralized platforms, and secure networks can be the lifeline for any resistance movement. Leverage technology to organize, communicate, and act swiftly. Understand cybersecurity protocols, and always be vigilant about digital hygiene to mitigate risks.

Legal and institutional battles are another front in this struggle. Courtrooms have historically been pivotal in preserving individual liberties. Engage with legal experts, support constitutional challenges, and stay informed about your rights. Proactive legal defenses often spell the difference between fleeting freedom and long-lasting autonomy. Familiarize yourself with the issues at hand and don't hesitate to seek legal redress when necessary. Even small victories in court can set significant precedents.

Allied and coalition-building efforts cannot be overlooked. Historically, international coalitions have been successful in curbing authoritarian ambitions. Identify potential global allies who share a common goal of preserving freedom. Engage in dialogues across borders and promote a unified front against overreaching agendas. These coalitions can offer resources, share strategies, and provide moral support.

Equally important is the necessity for resilience and mental fortitude. The path to preserving freedom is often fraught with setbacks. Psychological resilience among activists is as crucial as strategic planning. Understanding the psychological aspects can help activists deal with burnout and maintain long-term commitments. Encourage self-care and mutual support within your groups to sustain morale.

Finally, instill the values of freedom and autonomy in future generations. Educating young people about the importance of personal and collective freedoms can ensure that the fight is carried on. Foster critical thinking and encourage questioning attitudes among the youth—these are the seeds of long-term resistance.

Building a sustainable fight for freedom not only requires effort and dedication but also a multifaceted approach. By combining grassroots mobilization, technological savvy, legal action, international coalitions, psychological resilience, and intergenerational education, we can forge a robust resistance to the encroachments of the 2030 Agenda. The journey is complex, but the rewards are crucial. Engage, adapt, and persist.

Long-term Strategies

Building a sustained fight for freedom in the face of the 2030 Agenda requires a well-thought-out approach. To maintain momentum and ensure success, any strategy needs to be both robust and adaptable. Today's transient outbursts of resistance won't suffice; a structured, long-lasting plan is essential.

First, we must focus on education. Knowledge is a powerful tool in the battle against oppression. Informing the public about the potential dangers and consequences of the 2030 Agenda is a crucial step. This includes shedding light on what these policies truly entail and how they may impact personal freedoms and societal structures. Grassroots campaigns, online platforms, and community gatherings can be instruments for spreading this critical information.

Legal avenues are equally important. History shows that sustained legal battles can lead to substantial changes. Organizing a coalition of proactive lawyers and legal experts to challenge the policies associated with the 2030 Agenda can be a game-changer. Focusing on constitutional rights and challenging overreaching government policies through legal frameworks helps set precedents that can protect individual freedoms. It's not just about fighting current battles but about creating long-term safeguards.

Another long-term strategy involves building alliances across borders. The 2030 Agenda is a global initiative, and resistance to it must be global as well. International coalitions and alliances can pool resources, share strategies, and provide mutual support. Forming strong networks with like-minded organizations and individuals across the world strengthens the resistance and provides a unified front against the push towards global governance.

Economic independence also plays a vital role. Encouraging small businesses and local entrepreneurship helps decentralize power and makes communities more resilient to global mandates. Supporting local economies not only reduces reliance on centralized, potentially oppressive systems but also fosters a sense of community and solidarity.

The role of technology cannot be underestimated. Leveraging technological advancements to create secure, decentralized systems for communication and finance can counteract the push towards centralized controls. Blockchain technology, for instance, offers a way to manage transactions and data in a decentralized manner, reducing the risk of surveillance and control by centralized authorities.

Community resilience is also a key component of any long-term strategy. Building strong, self-reliant communities that can operate independently of centralized systems provides a buffer against loss of freedom. This includes everything from local food production and energy solutions to robust community governance structures.

Public perception and media influence are battlefronts that shouldn't be ignored. Long-term resistance can be aided by shifting public opinion. Utilizing alternative media channels to counter mainstream narratives helps in gathering support and informing a broader audience. Strategic use of social media, podcasts, blogs, and independent news outlets can propagate an alternative narrative, questioning and challenging the dominant discourse.

An effective long-term strategy also includes the cultivation of a robust civil society. Civil society organizations, including NGOs, advocacy groups, and think tanks, provide a sustained push-back against policies that threaten personal freedoms. These organizations not only advocate for change but also hold those in power accountable.

Activism is another pillar in this long-term strategy. Organizing regular, sustained actions, be they protests, petitions, or public forums, keeps the issue in public discourse. Keeping the momentum through coordinated efforts ensures the agenda's potential repercussions remain at the forefront of public consciousness.

Adaptability is crucial for any long-term strategy. The political and social landscape is continuously shifting, and so too must our strategies. By staying vigilant and responsive to changes, opportunities, and threats, we can adapt our approaches to continue effectively countering the 2030 Agenda's influence.

Lastly, we must keep hope alive. Sustaining a fight for freedom requires a collective belief in the possibility of a different, freer future. Inspirational leadership, unyielding commitment, and the belief that change is possible are all integral to sustaining long-term efforts. We must foster a culture where freedom and personal autonomy are valued and protected by all.

Mobilizing for Impact

Understanding the magnitude of the 2030 Agenda and its potential impact on our freedoms is merely the first step. To ensure a sustainable fight for freedom, mobilizing effectively and strategically is essential.

It's crucial to ground our efforts in realistic goals and actionable steps, while galvanizing support from various sectors of society. This multi-faceted approach will enable us to build a cohesive and resilient front against the encroachments on our personal liberties.

The key to mobilization is information. Knowledge is, and always has been, a powerful tool for instigating change. By disseminating well-researched, factual information about the 2030 Agenda and its implications, we can raise awareness on a broad scale. Whether it's through grassroots educational campaigns, social media activism, or community engagement, the objective is to inform as many people as possible about the stakes involved. A well-informed public is more likely to take meaningful action.

Social media platforms can be both allies and adversaries in this endeavor. On one hand, they provide a means to reach millions almost instantaneously. Platforms like Twitter, Facebook, and Instagram can spread messages virally, drawing attention to vital issues and mobilizing large groups of people. On the other hand, these platforms can also censor information and suppress dissenting voices. Navigating this terrain requires skill, vigilance, and alternative strategies, such as decentralized platforms or in-person networking.

Another strategic element involves coalition-building. Mobilizing for impact isn't a solo endeavor; it requires the collaboration and unity of various groups. From civil liberty organizations to local community groups, the formation of alliances strengthens the movement. These coalitions enhance resource-sharing, magnify advocacy efforts, and provide a larger platform for voicing concerns. Working together, disparate organizations can present a unified front, making it harder for opponents to dismiss or undermine our objectives.

Grassroots movements often serve as the backbone of impactful mobilization efforts. These movements are generally more agile, passionate, and closer to the community's heartbeats. They can quickly organize protests, disseminate pamphlets, and hold town hall meetings to not only spread awareness but also galvanize immediate action. Grassroots mobilization offers a bottom-up approach, which directly involves and empowers individuals within communities.

Financial resources, or the lack thereof, can also influence the success of mobilization efforts. Funding is often necessary for organizing events, producing educational materials, and supporting advocacy campaigns. Crowdfunding platforms, donor contributions, and grants from supportive organizations can aid in sustaining these initiatives. Transparency in fund allocation ensures continued public trust and engagement.

Education, both formal and informal, plays a pivotal role in mobilization. School curriculums, community workshops, and open forums can teach the implications of the 2030 Agenda. Educators, researchers, and activists should develop materials that lay out these concerns in an accessible, compelling manner. By bringing these issues into the educational system, we can prepare younger generations to understand and resist future encroachments on their freedoms.

While education arms the public with information, leadership directs the momentum. Effective leadership is essential for mobilizing large-scale, sustained actions. Leaders articulate visions, strategize actions, and inspire participation. Charismatic individuals who can rally people and clearly communicate the stakes involved can make or break a movement. Finding and nurturing such leaders within communities is indispensable for long-term success.

Media coverage, another crucial element, can amplify the scope and impact of mobilization efforts. Engaging with mainstream and alternative media ensures that the message reaches diverse audiences. Media involvement not only serves to inform but also legitimizes the movement. Coverage of peaceful protests, public forums, and educational initiatives can help galvanize broader support.

Legal tools and advocacy are fundamental components of any strategic mobilization plan. Understanding constitutional rights and leveraging them to challenge policies that threaten freedom can serve as powerful deterrents against the overreach of the 2030 Agenda. Legal organizations can assist in filing lawsuits, drafting petitions, and developing policy recommendations. Persistent legal challenges can slow down or even halt implementing draconian measures.

Finally, it's vital to recognize that mobilization is a continuous effort. Short-term victories are essential, but the ultimate goal is to sustain long-term resistance. Mobilizing for impact is not about episodic outbursts of activity but about creating a persistent, ever-evolving movement. Periodic assessments and adaptability ensure that strategies remain effective and aligned with goals.

The fight for freedom against the overarching ambitions of the 2030 Agenda requires a comprehensive, well-coordinated mobilization effort. Combining the power of information, coalition-building, grassroots movements, financial support, education, leadership, media engagement, and legal tools can carve out a robust path toward preserving our freedoms. The time is ripe for action, and through strategic mobilization, we can build a sustainable fight for freedom that endures for generations.

Conclusion

As we have navigated through the many facets of the 2030 Agenda, one thing is abundantly clear: it brings with it significant concerns about personal freedoms, privacy, and autonomy. The meticulously orchestrated plans laid out in the Agenda, from digital ID systems to central bank digital currencies (CBDCs), encapsulate a vision of top-down control that threatens the very fabric of individual liberty and economic freedom that many hold dear.

The 2030 Agenda is a tapestry interwoven with initiatives that may seem beneficial on the surface but, upon closer scrutiny, reveal a different story. The move toward a cashless society, exemplified by the rise of CBDCs, illustrates a troubling trend of increased state control over personal finances. With the potential to monitor and dictate how individuals spend their money, the implications are vast and deeply unsettling.

Moreover, the introduction of social credit systems, initially implemented in China, showcases a model where behavior is meticulously tracked and evaluated. This brings forth a reality where freedom of movement, speech, and even personal choices are subject to scrutiny and punishment. The erosion of personal freedom happening incrementally can ultimately lead to a complete loss of autonomy.

The role of powerful figures and organizations, such as Klaus Schwab and the World Economic Forum (WEF), serves as a stark reminder of the influence unelected bodies can wield on a global scale. These entities push an agenda that often bypasses democratic processes, imposing policies that may not align with the will of the general populace. The comfort zones of personal ownership and economic stability seem to vanish in the shadow of such movements, forcing a reevaluation of what it means to be truly free.

Canadian politicians, among others, play crucial roles in propagating the 2030 Agenda. Their involvement brings the debate closer to home, raising pertinent questions about national sovereignty and policy direction. As these political figures endorse and enforce the Agenda, it becomes imperative for citizens to question and challenge the motivations driving such endorsements.

Surveillance and digital tracking once belonged to dystopian fiction. Now, they are inching closer to reality. With each passing day, technology companies gather more data, painting a comprehensive picture of our lives. This encroachment on privacy has profound implications, not just for individual rights but also for the broader societal structure. The fear of constant surveillance can lead to self-censorship and deter dissent, creating a more conformist society at the expense of diversity and freedom of expression.

The landscape of education is also shifting in ways that prime future generations to accept these changes as the norm. Curricular changes aimed at promoting global citizenship and sustainability might seem benign but often serve as indoctrination tools, conditioning young minds to uncritically accept the 2030 Agenda. The critical thinking and individuality that are hallmarks of a free society risk being overshadowed by a homogenous global narrative.

In the economic realm, small businesses and entrepreneurs are under significant threat. The consolidation of power in the hands of big corporations, often facilitated by favorable policies, stifles innovation and restricts economic mobility. Independent businesses, which are the backbone of a thriving and diverse economy, struggle to compete against the monopolistic tendencies endorsed by the 2030 Agenda.

Resistance movements and legal battles emerge as beacons of hope, demonstrating that there still are people willing to fight for personal freedoms and constitutional rights. These efforts, while often faced with significant challenges, are crucial in pushing back against the overreach of global governance structures. Public perception, largely shaped by media narratives, plays a crucial role in either bolstering or undermining these resistance efforts. The media's role in framing the discourse cannot be overstated; it has the power to either enlighten the public or lead it astray.

Moving forward, international coalitions against the 2030 Agenda demonstrate that united efforts can make a substantial difference. Collaboration across borders creates a strong front that can effectively challenge and counteract restrictive policies. These alliances are essential in preserving the liberties that face the greatest risk under the 2030 Agenda.

Looking to the future, the projections and scenarios paint contrasting pictures of what lies ahead. While some outcomes suggest deeper entrenchment of control and loss of freedoms, others offer hope for better awareness and preparation. Mobilizing for impact requires a long-term approach that balances immediate action with sustainable strategies for preserving freedom.

Ultimately, building a sustainable fight for freedom demands more than just reactionary measures; it requires proactive and thoughtful strategies that encompass all societal facets – economic, political, and cultural. Only by understanding the full scope of the 2030 Agenda can we effectively counter its encroachments and safeguard the principles of personal freedom and democracy.

As we close this detailed examination of the 2030 Agenda, it's crucial to remain vigilant and engaged. The fight for freedom is not a series of isolated battles but an ongoing effort that requires commitment, resilience, and an unwavering dedication to fundamental liberties. The choices we make today will shape the future landscape of personal freedoms for generations to come.

Appendix A:
Appendix

Within this appendix, readers will find supplementary information and additional resources to better understand the themes and topics discussed throughout the book. This section serves as an aid, offering further clarity and context to the arguments and observations made in the main chapters. Below is an organized list of various components included in this appendix.

Glossary of Key Terms

Throughout the book, various terms and jargon have been used to explain complex ideas, policies, and technologies. This glossary provides definitions and explanations of these key terms to ensure a deeper comprehension:

- **2030 Agenda:** A global plan adopted by all United Nations Member States in 2015 to achieve sustainable development goals by 2030.

- **CBDC (Central Bank Digital Currency):** A digital form of central bank money that could be used as a medium of exchange, store of value, and unit of account.

- **WEF (World Economic Forum):** An international organization for public-private cooperation that engages political, business, and other leaders to shape global, regional, and industry agendas.

- **Digital ID:** An electronic identification system that could be used for accessing government services, banking, and other essential services.

Notable Figures

This section highlights key individuals who have garnered influence in the discussion of the 2030 agenda and its implications:

1. **Klaus Schwab:** Founder and executive chairman of the World Economic Forum, known for promoting the idea of the Great Reset.

2. **Bill Gates:** Co-founder of Microsoft and philanthropist, influential in public health and sustainability initiatives.

3. **Justin Trudeau:** Prime Minister of Canada, plays a significant role in advancing the agenda within Canadian policies.

Additional Resources

For those looking to delve deeper into the subject matter, here is a curated list of books, articles, and documentaries:

- *"The Great Reset: And the War for the World"* by Alex Jones – A book that explores the unfolding global agenda and its potential impact.

- *"COVID-19: The Great Reset"* by Klaus Schwab and Thierry Malleret – A foundational text outlining the concepts behind the Great Reset.

- *"China's Surveillance State: A Pathway to Power"* by John Battelle – An article examining how China's social credit system could influence global practices.

- *"1984"* (Documentary) – A powerful visual portrayal of the implications of a surveillance state.

This appendix aims to provide a comprehensive overview and serve as a quick reference guide for terms, notable figures, and resources discussed in the book. Together, these elements will hopefully offer readers a more thorough understanding of the significant and often alarming aspects of the 2030 agenda.

www.ingramcontent.com/pod-product-compliance
Lightning Source LLC
Chambersburg PA
CBHW020315290526
45785CB00007B/2798